What do you think of when you see...

Who do you think of when you see...

Come and see who, what, where, and why...

See the images in motion at
www.TheSignOnHalfDome.com

THE SIGN
On Half Dome

Landmark Evidence About God
sure to change your life

Written by

Bruce Ebinger

Published by Infinite Ripple, San Francisco, California

The Sign on Half Dome: Landmark Evidence About God

By Bruce Ebinger

www.thesignonhalfdome.com

Published by:
Infinite Ripple
PO Box 27065
San Francisco, CA 94127
info@infiniteripple.com

Printed in the United States of America

ISBN-13: 978-0-9794536-0-1
ISBN-10: 0-9794536-0-7

Acknowledgements

My friends, who are crucial support to my life, are deeply prized. You help me keep my composure, and sharpen my spirit beyond anything I would be capable of alone. I could only begin to hope I've been as valuable to you as you've been to me. Bill and Yvonne, you are especially unwavering pillars of support and guidance. Bill's feedback contributed to the shape of this book, and ultimately to my own life. I love you both.

My family remains a source of strength. My Gramma who's no longer with us; Cathy and Greg (mom and dad), who show a true spirit of sacrifice and love; to Jenny, my second mom who has been a rock of reason and practicality; and my brother Adam whose life has proven to be a deep well of great fortune—even from his wheelchair. To all my brothers and sisters, you enrich my life. I want to thank my cousin Paul who has provided a second set of eyes throughout the years for me in seeing the images contained in this book—your friendship encourages me.

And, to my dear wife, who loved me through this intense journey of bringing this work to its implementation. I was kept balanced, and most of all, humble, which helped add significance to each word. Our marriage has made life all the more genuine, and taught me far more than if I had been without. You've reminded me, and continue to, of the more important things in life—love and intimacy, to which you do exceedingly well. You are faithful and true. To our precious little girl, whose presence opens up a whole new world of revelation and love I couldn't have imagined. And even to our new one on the way, who encourages me to prepare for more love. You all add a wealth of great fortune to my life.

Foreword

I was not expecting to be so moved while working on an editing project, but Bruce's personal and spiritual journey inspired me. As I read, I found myself reflected in his words and his passion encouraged me to re-engage and continue working on my own relationship with God. My spiritual journey was abandoned back in my 20's, trading it in for a more "here-and-now" mentality. Bruce's book challenged my own thinking and I thank him for jarring me out of my comfortable mental and spiritual state of being. Whether or not you agree or believe whole-heartedly with Bruce's perspectives, his book will certainly move you or at least make you want to debate life's big questions.

I have to admit that I did not look at the pictures while I read through Bruce's draft. I deliberately chose not to look at them while I edited. I felt I could focus more on Bruce's words to ensure that he was clearly conveying his message rather than relying solely on the pictures. I am so glad I waited to look at the pictures because Bruce's words are powerful and do fully stand on their own. I have since examined his pictures and found them to be compelling and fascinating, his words inspiring me the most.

I was fortunate enough to grow up about an hour from Yosemite and have hiked and camped extensively there my entire life. Before I ever knew Bruce or began working on this editing project, I have loved Yosemite. Its grandeur and beauty have always inspired me every time I am there, cleansing and renewing my soul. Personally, Yosemite has a knack of recharging my batteries and making me realize what life is all about. Now that I don't live as close to Yosemite, I'm still able to visit over a weekend, returning to my life in the City with a renewed sense of energy.

I have even climbed to the top of Half Dome, and now realize that I never actually looked at its face close enough to see the images Bruce describes. After working on this project, I have since looked through my own personal photographs of Half Dome with amazement at how clearly I now see these images. It is astonishing that they were always there but I just never saw them. This makes me laugh because it is so characteristic of our treatment of God in general, not looking hard enough to see or listening close enough to hear. Bruce's book has made me begin looking and listening with more effort. How much more is out there for me to see if only I open my eyes and heart and mind more?

I must disclose that Bruce and Stephani Ebinger are also personal friends of mine. Although I am a closer friend to his wife Stephani (interns together in Washington D.C. while in college over 10 years ago), Bruce and I have slowly gotten to know each other over the years. From what I have learned about him, I know that Bruce is one of the most conscientious, kind and diplomatic men I know. He also lives by his principles and beliefs, which is rare in this day and age. He is an extremely hard worker, diligent and persistent, as well as a dedicated father and loving husband.

If Bruce's personal journey and the following story do not inspire you, then I know the topics he touches upon in this book will certainly challenge you to begin thinking about them. You may have diametrically opposing viewpoints, you may form your own conclusions, but better yet, you may begin to improve upon your own relationship with God. It's been a pleasure working on this book and I hope you enjoy reading it as much as I did.

Courtnee Riise Averskog
Marin County, California

Disclaimer

This book is designed to increase awareness about reality. It is sold with the understanding that the publisher and author are not engaged in any specific political agenda, or agenda affiliated any particular religious organization. This book is merely a presentation of facts that are directed to their source.

Information contained here is meant to be used in constructive ways, and not for destructive purposes. The author and publisher advocate the positive, constructive, non-violent, merciful, life-respecting, and loving use of the content within these covers, but are neither responsible for their success or failure. Disrespect, hate, criminal activity, vandalism, violence, murder, oppression, terrorism, and war are diametrically opposed to the author and publisher's intent, and are emphatically not endorsed herein.

The truth about one aspect of life may, at times, deem another aspect untrue. The objective of the author Bruce Ebinger and Infinite Ripple is not to disprove anything, but to articulate that which is found to be true. If in the process something is shown to be true or untrue, we are released from liability of whatever effect it may have on everything affiliated with that "something".

Great effort and attempt has been made to insure the accuracy of the content of this book. There may be, however, aspects disagreed with. This book contains information about cultural elements and archeology up to the printed date. Prophecy has been sited, and it's source given, which the author and Infinite Ripple release itself from full liability.

The purpose of this book is to share a new discovery with the public, and help interpret how it relates to existing facts and other written work. The author and Infinite Ripple shall have neither liability nor responsibility to any person or entity with respect to any loss or damage caused or alleged to be caused directly or indirectly by the information contained in this book.

If you do not wish to be bound by the above, please do not purchase this book, or return to the publisher for a refund.

CONTENTS

Chapter One

On Your Mark

"There are two ways to live;
one is as though nothing is a miracle. The other is as if everything is."
– Albert Einstein

On a day like any other, we talk the afternoon away. Grassy, green hills, a breeze made to soothe the skin, and plenty of people enjoying the serene atmosphere; Sandra and I go on about nothing in particular. We used to work together at the local grocery store, and hadn't talked for some time. Other people are playing with their dogs, riding bikes, and enjoying the day like us. This perfect day intoxicates the senses.

Sandra on the grass across from me, my left arm propping my head, I pick and toss blades of grass. I could easily fall asleep it's so comfortable, just lounging on my side. The beautiful sky, partly full with stark white, puffy clouds, and its bold, blue backdrop, begin to capture my attention.

I notice a certain cloud with a small, round hole having a tiny black spot directly in the center. As far up as the eye could see, I lock my sight on this spec of an object and watch it grow. I soon realize this spec isn't actually growing—it's coming closer! The closer it comes the more the clouds open up around it. I sense something of great magnitude happening. Excitement and anxiousness come over me all at once. "It's here! It's here! It's time!" I yell, now jumping up and down.

This object in the sky comes closer and closer as the clouds keep opening, and I begin making out the hovering entity in the sky. Finally, almost directly overhead, but far enough away, I can see three sides—the bottom and two edges. From my vantage point, this whole mass seems to now rest a couple miles above the earth, occupying a great majority of the sky, with its shadow now covering the area. I look around for Sandra, but don't see her. I immediately look back up and continue observing, making out a large stone mass dominating the atmosphere.

This hovering rock displays a caramel-like color, like the kind of light brown stone you would find in a river—wet and shiny, with various shades. It makes me think of a building block, but with smoothed edges, and crags, having undulating surfaces, and places with shadows. The whole thing is a quarter thick as it is wide, but having a square-like mass. This slab of rock is intertwined with streams of cloud, weaving and circulating through it as if alive, and breathing. I've never even considered such a site! I feel the need to somehow be on top of this stone, but I'm not sure exactly why I feel this, or just how to get there. So many different emotions are coursing through me.

As I continue to stare, now I see seven streamlined cloud figures—like birds with no wings, descending out of the great stone. They are small in comparison to the rock and sky, but could be as big as giant jets compared to me. I can't tell! They soar down in pairs, tightly knit, but apart from the other pairs who follow. Lastly, a single cloud figure descends alone. Like soaring eagles, these seven volts of cloud circle all the way down behind a hill, but I never see them touch the ground. I look back into the sky to see the clouds already closing to cover this site. And I never heard a sound…

I grieve, and feel as though I've missed something, or missed a chance, or some opportunity. Do I not hear what I am supposed to hear? How should I be responding to all of this? I look back up into the cloud filled sky and ask, "What should I do?" Still nothing. I turn to see a group of people standing around, and begin to ask, "Did you see it? You? Or you?" One person says no, but another, yes. "No? How could you not see it? It was right there in the sky!" I exclaim! "How about you?" I ask another. He replies, "Yes, I saw it!" I go on, "And you? What about you?" As some nod yes, amazingly others, no.

The Reason for Writing

Over the years I toiled for the best way to tell of my personal journey leading to a remarkable eyewitness account exposing our true reality. It is extremely valuable to me for you to understand why I've written this book. An open and honest search for the truth about God was forged in part by pushing back at my own fear and inner conflicts that were holding me hostage from a greater understanding about the essence of life. This personal process unleashed an avalanche of answers—real answers, concrete answers, answers revealed in stone. This proved to be life changing. Faithful or skeptic, you can't avoid becoming part of this report. Even if your convictions are strong, be challenged, be sharpened, but don't allow yourself to overlook the obvious. This book is a constructive exploration of life's core, using common sense, evidence-based facts, and your own assessment to answer an ancient yearning: to know if life is a result of random chance, or whether intelligent design determines our purpose. No one is being asked to suspend his or her critical faculties and trust blindly. Some of the most sought after questions about God are answered here once and for all. New, striking evidence has been found. This new discovery will affect the way you view your life.

It was Socrates who said, "The unexamined life is not worth living." I concur, and also encourage all to examine life more closely, more objectively. This book is a simple, yet crucial inspection of reality. I felt the strong need to clarify the difference between subjective and objective truth, because "truth" in general is widely misunderstood. In turn, this leads to a clear understanding about what will happen when we die, articulated by the real consequences and implications of life itself. By confirming the nature of objective truth at the outset of this book, the reality in which we find ourselves will be clearly understood. Some may be saying, "Subjective and objective truth don't really matter much to me. Why bother with this?" And beyond this you might not even care to know whether or not God exists. And further, "If I did know," you might think, "It still wouldn't change the way I live anyway. What's the ultimate good in knowing? I'm fine with what I believe already." But the question remains, are you really? Are *we*?

In the 14th Century, a deadly pandemic known as the Black Death began claiming millions and millions of lives, and continued its strike year after year. Since then, because humankind took action to educate itself about the reality of this disease, society has worked fervently to prevent catastrophic plague by way of vaccines, antibiotics, and insecticides. The key motivator to making such essential advancement has been survival, and the desire itself to progress. The ultimate good that came out of fervently examining this ravaging disease was the very triumph over it. The continued exploration and advancements to improve and save human lives persistently raises the quality of life, extending our time on earth. It matters more than one could quantify that we engage those things that would enrich and prolong our life, even existence. Today, like the Black Death, there is an epidemic of the mind, unawareness about reality that threatens the unity, progress, and well being of humankind. This book has been written to share striking, and specific evidence that will help anyone who desires to know the truth identify reality in the most absolute way. This account presents an opportunity for unity among all people. Needed and necessary change could be embraced even though we might be accustomed to our ingrained, familiar ways.

With the potential for a re-ignited nuclear weapons proliferation, and the always-looming international confrontation over resources, ideals, and territory, unity is an ever-precious resource we're not fighting hard enough for. The need for humankind to become wiser, and more aware of this dimension we live in is our primary hope for reaching true peace. These pages answer whether or not religious faith is a cultural virus actually standing in the way of true enlightenment, or whether distrust in God proves to be more dangerous. As infants, before any one of us learns to speak, the desire to communicate comes *before* we communicate. With persistence, we one day gain the knowledge and capacity to be able to express our mind. Our "will" helps to open the way to knowledge and revelation. The yearning to want to know the truth, to continuously learn, leads to the true answers about reality. And the truth we discover is meant to guide our everyday living by encouraging the best solutions to the many global and personal struggles we all face—alone and together.

Ambiguity about life and death can be transformed into vital purpose. *The Sign on Half Dome* shows how we can be as certain about the supernatural as we are about our earthly responsibilities. By understanding the difference between subjective and objective truth, at the very least you will become smarter, and sharper. By desiring to know and pursue the universal truth about reality, you will, in turn observe it. You must want to know the answers before they will come. As humans, we are alive to progress, so progress we must. This is what's unfolding.

This book will demonstrate how to objectively understand the whole of reality—the spiritual or philosophical side, God or the universe. The truth will come to a precise head. Perhaps the world and our many different religions and philosophies conflict because we aren't objective enough with our approach. Perhaps part of our self becomes lost in the process. By reading on, more of who you are, and how to better know your life purpose will be established. At this point,

I'm not saying whether or not I think God is real. This account will speak for itself by way of physical evidence, making clear how to embrace what is truly real. My own personal worldview will unfold. You will be able to confirm the true reality for yourself—who or what God is, if God is.

If you have questions like: What matters most? What are the answers to life's deepest questions? Should I search for answers? Do I think knowing even matters? Is the world becoming a worse place with its end drawing near, or does each generation trick itself into believing so? Along the way they will be answered. I know when I look at the world, and all its sufferings and strife, I see a world raging with itself and searching for peace, while uncertain of how to attain—ultimately rejecting the truth it desperately needs to bring resolution. Compassion and mercy is longed for by so many amidst this struggle, this war between good and evil, between greed and graciousness. This book addresses this tug of war we find ourselves in, and explains what to do about it, even how to make peace. The discovery contained herein illuminates our role—our personal journey upon the stage of life.

I've often asked if there's some great cosmic "point" to life I'm supposed to get. I just want to live according to whether there is or isn't one. This longing to know if I have a purpose and destiny has burdened me greatly, and setting out to discover has been a voyage leading to certainty and understanding defining our common ground. I questioned, wrestled, and comprehended—but mostly, I searched with sincerity. The honest truth is what matters, and what we do about it matters even more. This book will show what is true, and shares what can be done in light of it. Finding truth above untested conviction and obtaining knowledge over feelings has been the priority here.

I must admit "the truth" can be personally daunting, and so broad, bringing about the wonder if signs from heaven enlighten, or if sheer imaginations are merely misleading us. These pages provide reason along with the accounts of others about the "supernatural" realm. Together, we have the opportunity to comprehend an amazing encounter, and explore a revelation exposing the specific truth about the other dimension, and our connection to it. How sure are you about what you believe, why you breathe, or what true love is, or the purpose of life—of my mine, of yours? I know for me, I want concrete answers about this, but honestly wanting to know can be a struggle. At some level, it's intimidating.

These questions and struggles have been my own. I learned that those answers, known or unknown, make up my worldview about the origin of life—God creating everything, or everything coming from random chance. In light of this, our personal worldview greatly shapes the way we live. Our worldviews collectively form the cultures that govern us. This makes our world what it is—positive or negative, at peace or in conflict. Our world is the way it is because of what we individually profess and/or live out. Therefore, the worldview you and I hold is of crucial importance. We can either wrestle against each other or come to understand our common ground, and unite upon it. We must be willing to meet each other at truth and understanding if true peace and extraordinary bounds are ever to be attained. The truth is the true middle ground—the common ground.

Therefore, it is vital that each one of us understands our own worldview, and the worldviews of others. We will then comprehend how we actually influence the world. This book is a tool that will lead you to things that are true, to build upon a stable foundation that will span generations—a foundation of genuine health and wellness. Let your mind be challenged, and your heart be tested while the deepest answers reveal who we are.

Strangely enough, our fingertips are brushing over pictures, over words, holding answers to intense yearnings. I came to find that my eyes give passing glances to wondrous sights and sheer amazements (call them miracles if you will), while I am unaware, and that pieces of life's puzzle are within everyone. You know it! You feel it! Obscurity about this must be unlocked in order to light the mysteries of life. Great truth is in our midst. We can know the origin of life. You are about to embark upon an expedition where doubt and uncertainty about life and ourselves stand no match for your honest desire to observe true reality. Even those who feel bold already will be emboldened all the more. Come and see how a true and awesome wonder of staggering precision testified by nature leads us to our common ground, able to strengthen our world.

This personal account shares the unearthing of a physical phenomenon. This event distills life down to our common ground, revealing our ultimate origin, implicating powerful justice. It teaches of our nature and clarifies why—why life is the way it is. Perhaps you believe you know why. This will deepen it still. Great love reveals itself. You will better understand your individual value. Life-purpose will be clearer, and a glimpse into the future will be taken.

This book is not meant to act as judge and jury of anyone's soul, or heart, or mind, and dash hope away. It is meant as a vehicle of understanding—a treasure chest of encouragement. Many optimistically seek the spiritual in hopes of gaining, at the very least, a glimpse of eternal life. This has been part of my path and desire to know what is really true. How many of us hope our lives will be good enough, full of meaning and purpose? Some venture to rest on the concept that life is just what you see, and spiritual beings are delusional because they do not exist beyond this realm. So many things hoped for by so vast a number. Hope should be placed in what is real. This book addresses our many ambitions and aspirations. When I look into the truth I can see my reflection, and everything surrounding me in it. It's amazing! And I'm not alone. The face of reality and life's genuine essence are gathered together in these pages to see.

This may sound somewhat hazy, but things will become unmistakable. I've come to appreciate that seeking and knowing the authentic reality, the objective truth, is the greatest path I could have ever embarked. The contents within these covers tell the story about my great care to know the truth about life and shares what has been found. The truth and its intensity has changed me. Positive power and personal growth waits to be unchained within every individual alive. Let's reach for whatever strength is within us, and move away from the fears that hold us back from being more of who we truly are—who we know we are meant to be. Life is too short to spend in bondage—physical, emotional, spiritual, or you name it. The truth exists to set us free. We are alive in order to grow. This book contains powerful truth that will at the very least stir you deeply.

This personal account is told starting at the point in time after I graduated high school, but before I was twenty years old. I want these events to unfold to you as they unfolded to me. I started writing this account at the age of twenty-two. This book spans about twenty-four years of my life, with most of the content concentrated around the age of twenty-one. The Epilogue catches us up to the present day. Bringing this book to you has most definitely been a personal journey, labored with utmost sincerity. My hope is for you to walk along with me, and observe these things in your own way.

However bold, however small; listen with me for life's perpetual voice. Please join me on my search for the ultimate truth about life. No one is excluded. This "face to face" meeting with reality will explain the reasons why we are all here, on earth. Perhaps this is a good look at another world we've been hoping for.

You will know it when you see it! I'm not attempting to convince you to believe in ambiguous notions or great fantasy. You will be able to show and tell others of your findings, and even touch them. Personal transformation leading to positive, global change through our common ground waits in the wings. A great roar is in place to sound.

Chapter Two

The Search

"The clearest way into the universe
is through a forest wilderness."
– John Muir

The rock in the sky was a dream. It was the kind, when you wake from, you feel like you'd never gone to sleep. It was the kind that had me wondering: was it real, or was I in some different dimension, in some other place? I'm not sure how to explain it, but I can still taste those images, and that magnificent afternoon with its perfect breeze. This dream came to me after my encounter in Yosemite Valley. To some degree, I realize the dream has something to do with what I see in Yosemite, and happened near the time I first saw. But still, that dream was eerily real. There was even more beyond my exchange with the other people in my dream, images that I don't feel I'm ready to share. Was it all in my head, or am I to take away a greater significance? To this day, I'm still processing the events that filled my mind's eye while I slept. It greatly impacts me, and if anything, has helped fuel my passion to write this book.

So what qualifies me to write about such a huge subject—reality that is? Good question. When I start to think I know, I realize perhaps, I don't. As you read, you will begin to understand my search. Perhaps the reasons will stand out. In 1970 I was born in the city of San Francisco. My parents were very young, and lived on the infamous Ashbury Street in the Haight district. I couldn't really call them hippies, because by the time I was old enough to know what a hippy was, they weren't. But my mom did say she used to iron her long, dark hair. By the time my younger brother was just a toddler, my mom went her way, and my dad his. My mom, my brother, and I grew up in a neighborhood just a few miles south of San Francisco. My mother and Gramma basically raised us. Overall, I had a pretty stable childhood. We lived in the same house for about fifteen years until I moved out when I was nineteen. I remember our neighborhood being filled with lots of kids. We ran around doing all the sorts of things kids do. Our cousins lived a few houses down, and there never seemed to be a dull moment. I remember going into the hills with my brother and our friends to capture the biggest pumpkin spiders and silverbacks we could find to bring them home. A couple of times they escaped and I remember my mom finding them in her garden. She, however, was not pleasantly surprised.

I am fortunate for the life I had growing up. I also remember getting so muddy that my older cousins cleaned us up by hosing us down on the front lawn. Even in high school, through those difficult teen years, things went pretty well. But now that I think about it, if you asked my mom she might have another story. I know my Gramma always thought we were angels. Fortunately, her thoughts about us were more subjective than objective. We weren't really church-going people, but we'd go now and then. My mom and Gramma believe in God, and I remember my Gramma always had this certain picture of Jesus around, which always seemed to bug me. I thought he looked like a hippy. But she liked it, and I loved her.

My biological father became a born-again Christian by the time I was five or six, and then married a Christian woman after divorcing my mother. This became my other family who lived a couple hours away, just outside of Sacramento California. They eventually had three children. For many years, my brother and I would go visit for a couple of weeks during the summer. The swimming and meeting different people was always fun, but we didn't look forward to going to church—at least I didn't. When I was about eight, I remember my brother and I being baptized in someone's swimming pool. They asked us if we wanted to ask Jesus to be our lord and savior. We said yes, and were baptized. It seemed like I was doing it more for others than for myself. That was the religious pinnacle of my youth, if you'd call it that. From here, we didn't "live" as I understood Christians to live—mainly going to church every Sunday.

We just happened to be like most people we knew. We liked rock music and the popular bands from the 1980's. My born-again dad and his new Christian wife, however, did not. This was a major disconnect. As kids, it was still okay to see them occasionally, but we looked forward to getting back home to our life with mom. Fortunately, as I got older I chose to spend more and more time as a young adult with my dad and step-mom, getting to know them and my two brothers and sister on this side of my family. To this day, I'm very glad I did. I'm so grateful, and only wish I had spent more time with my brothers and sister growing up.

My mom remarried before I was a teenager to a man named Greg, with two children. As I entered the teenage years, I had bouts of rebellion towards my new steph-dad. It wasn't that he was abusive, or didn't like my brother and me. In fact, I remember doing fun things together. Some of it was my own internal frustrations which had nothing to do with him, and some just youthful defiance. I certainly did things that hurt him I'm not proud of. Fortunately as I grew older I learned to appreciate him being in my life, and have been grateful to have Greg as my father along with my new brother and sister. Over time I was happy to call him my dad. No one's perfect, but he has demonstrated great committment to our family to this day.

I pretty much see myself as an average person. I hope this doesn't bore you, but maybe it's the ordinary nature of my life that led to this intense revelation in Yosemite Valley. Maybe it's our familiarity that stands out, and because we might not be so different, you're just as qualified as me to search, and find even more. This might be the catch: when we start thinking we're too special, or something we're not then we get stuck in the rut of analyzing our self instead of simply looking and searching for the answers we want and need. The focus of my search seems to be less on me, and more on the big picture of reality.

After high school graduation, I remember having this aching burden to discover the "truth." I needed to know the truth about life to base the rest of *my* life upon. If there is a natural, moral code in motion, I needed to know if it's something I should be following. If not, I should be free to create my own set of standards. This point in my life marks an intense search for the "meaning of life." Pardon the cliché, but I sensed that there was more to life than meets the eye. More to life than working hard just to accumulate stuff—more to life than myself. I wanted to hear if life had something to say to me, if life is even able to speak. Maybe I just wanted to believe this. Either way, I had to know what is true. I began to believe that there is a "higher power", but was unsure of what to believe about it. Perhaps for all I really knew, it could have been my imagination. So I sought to confirm.

At that time, I began developing a love to engage in the deepest conversations about this subject. I felt it was helpful to hear someone else's point of view. I feel so fortunate that at such a young age, I was able to connect with people at this level. I still liked to go out and have fun, and take long hikes to places I've never been, or just hang out doing nothing. But I also looked forward to the times when the layers of everyday life would peel back, and I could delve into the great unknown—at least talk about it with others. Sometimes sparks flew, and other times I'd come away with more pieces to life's puzzle. Either way, I grew from those encounters.

Part of me wanted to confirm the ultimate truth about reality because I was frustrated with life's contradictions. I was frustrated with the religions I knew about, telling me, "You don't know God!" or "You are going to hell!" or even, "I'm going to heaven!" At least from my limited perspective, I wondered how they factually know this. It seemed to me that people of religion didn't really know for a fact what they thought was true, other than having faith in what they're saying was true. Maybe it's just me, but I'm still frustrated with answers based purely on faith and speculation. I want rational justification to form my worldview, representing reality instead of holding to an untested paradigm. This set in motion my strong desire to dissect reality. I decided to make it a quest to understand what the "truth" actually is. I wanted to put away the confusion, and know the truth about life, about God, about myself. Who am I really? Is God really there? I am banking on the truth to reveal the answer. And so I became driven to gain a deeper understanding about the nature of truth, and how to best understand it.

What is truth, really?

At this time in my life, not yet twenty years of age, literal truth is molding me through my very fascination of it. It's almost as if truth is calling me to find it—more of it! My personal confidence is being built as I seek how things actually exist. I have a growing appreciation for accuracy and exactness. For whatever reason, I'm intrigued. Now and then when I'm standing on a beach and stare out at the great blue in front of me, my mind wonders at how vast the depths of the ocean really are. I think, "Somewhere, a massive great whale is gracefully swimming deep below the surface. If I could be there I imagine it cold, dark, but real—a remarkable site and a myriad of sensations foreign to my everyday life. This place beneath the water is almost impossible for me to comprehend." Even sitting on my couch, my mind wanders to places like this, marveling at what is happening in our world at the very moment I sit and think about it. I also like to contemplate the synchronization of life, and picture myself surrounded by certain awesome, intensities. I can only guess about what is really going on millions of light years away inside this universe or on some other planet. Who really knows? But amazing things exist beyond what we can even begin to witness! We know, because when we observe remarkable events for the first time, we are in fact, amazed.

The surreal captivates me. So much wonder simultaneously existing, even pain and suffering, unfortunately. And no matter where I am, I know amazing things are literally happening. It's not easy for me to put into words, but I know where I am in time and space, and if God is real, God must be somewhere this very second. But *this* reality is something I'm not content sitting back to just imagine. I want to find it before I die! I want to know it. And if it truly exists, God that is, I want to see if God can be seen. I want to know the ultimate truth about reality.

Simple words in our vocabulary also mean important things, and my conversations with people about "truth" have demonstrated that there is some confusion. After a long, drawn out discussion one time, I was told, "The truth is whatever you or I want it to be." This to me was irrational! How far have we gotten away from our good ole common sense? I've always understood the truth to be a fact, or occurrence, or something that actually exists. Like in the court of law, you get sworn in to, "tell the truth, the whole truth, and nothing but the truth." If my friend who told me, "the truth is whatever you want it to be," was on the witness stand, he might end up committing perjury. Why? Because when we are told to tell the truth, people are asking to know exactly what happened, or what we know for certain. We are being asked to report the facts. If we account for the truth to be anything other than what is factual, the judge is ordered to throw us in the slammer. What you saw or heard is actually what you saw or heard, and this is the account we are asked to be truthful about—presenting the facts.

I've also been told, "Well, you have your truth, and I have mine." This point of our particular conversation was reached because of some things I said about life, and my opinion about the existence of God. I thought, "Okay, maybe I don't really know what I'm talking about here, but how could two, contradicting opinions or conclusions both be true at the same time?" For example, if my friend says God is this way, yet I say God does not exist, then how could the truth I claim and the truth he claims coexist? One of us has got to be off a bit. And then there's the time I'm talking to someone about God being real, but we have entirely different pictures—again, with major contradictions. It doesn't make sense to me how we can all have our own truth about reality. What about reality's truth? So my approach is to somehow let reality speak for itself, regardless of what I think.

Along my search I uncover two kinds of truth, and realize that many people are unclear about the basic meaning of truth—even me in all this. I'm beginning to understand why people claim their exclusive truth, while at the same time I see parts of the truth-determining process missing in some of us. To see eye to eye, we need to clarify. Think of the next several pages as a way to confirm we are talking apples to apples.

One kind of truth is subjective. The Merriam-Webster Online Dictionary lists a definition of subjective as:

> ...peculiar [or special] to a particular individual: personal...arising out of or identified by means of one's perception of one's own states and processes... lacking in reality or substance: illusory...*

The other kind of truth is objective, which is:

> ...of, relating to, or being an object, phenomenon, or condition in the realm of sensible experience independent of individual thought and perceptible by all observers: having reality independent of the mind <*objective reality*>...*

When *I* refer to "truth" hear me as meaning objective truth. This is the standard for observing God or reality I am going by. I'm talking truth. I'm talking facts. The kind you can observe for yourself. It's also important I acknowledge that many physical manifestations begin as subjective thoughts. We humans have the capacity to desire, and will our subjective thoughts and experiences to potentially become objective reality—buildings, art, expressions, and so on. In light of the nature of subjective thoughts and objective truth there are two possibilities: either

*   By permission. From the Merriam-Webster Online Dictionary©2007 by Merriam-Webster, Incorporated (www.Merriam-Webster.com). Reference http://www.m-w.com/dictionary/subjective, and http://www.m-w.com/dictionary/objective.

people can actually create or dismiss the reality of God with the power of thought (you having your truth and me having mine—even contradicting one another), or we can't create or dismiss reality because there is only one, objective actuality. I'm not a scientist, but I would guess both circumstances being possible seem highly, highly unlikely. So again I ask, what is really true?

I personally and simply just want to know the reality of our actual existence. And based on the line of objective thinking, for reality to be considered "actual existence," it must be perceivable by others *to* experience, or witness. It's true that thoughts are, in part, reality, but it's also true that thoughts don't always equal reality. A lie is a thought, but a false account equals *false* reality. Subjective truth is therefore not automatically equal to physical reality. I'm looking for the objective reality to display its objective truth.

Along with bias, perception has a tendency of being complicated when I try to perpetrate my subjective thoughts as physical truth, before they've been substantiated as an observable fact actually existing to other people. This is most likely where the friction between people with differing viewpoints originates. Proper substantiation of my subjective thoughts and perceptions can lead to objective truth—a condition in the realm of sensible experience independent of individual thought and perceptible by all observers, existing independent of the mind. Whether anyone is around to hear it, or not, a tree will make a sound when it hits the ground. This is objective truth. It exists apart from us. I look at it this way:

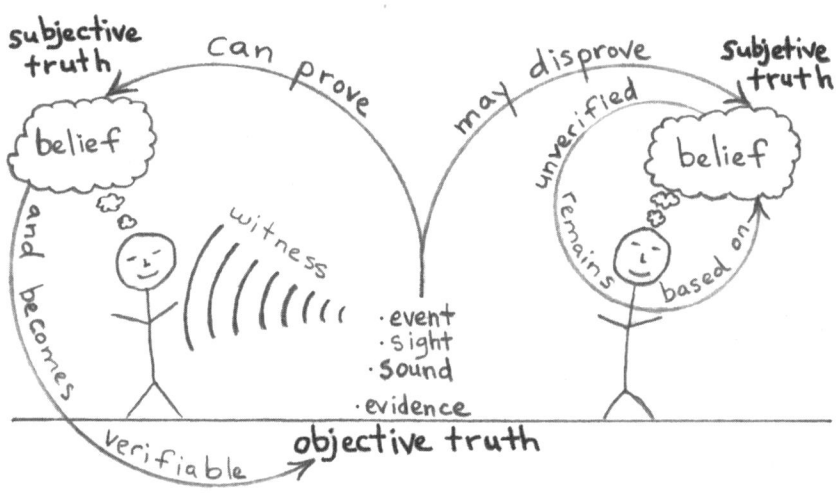

Simply put, subjective truth comes from within our hearts and minds, and objective truth is what surrounds us, existing regardless of what's in our mind, or even what I believe. Faith does not automatically make something real. Faith is only as good as the object our faith is placed in. It's when my subjective experience aligns with the objective environment that reality is then truly perceived—not always understood, but nonetheless apparent. I am now able to distinguish reality because I agree within my mind that the subjective and the objective align. Simply put, I witness the tree falling and internally concur the tree has fallen. This simple reality is now exposed. It is now recorded in my brain as fact, and is true for others whether they saw or heard the tree fall. It becomes truth or reality that the tree has fallen. And to confirm the alignment of my subjective with the objective, more than one witness begins the verification process. With this in mind, it becomes possible for things to be true for all people, in all places, at all times. Again, this is the standard by which I am going by to witness the true essence of the universe, or even God. But is it really possible to confirm the reality of God in this way?

Please don't hear me ruling out love as *not* being truth because it can't be physically seen, other than its manifested acts of love. Love is powerful and significant beyond measure, and most definitely true. Benevolence, charity, the nurturing of children, and showing great kindness to others are just a few physical manifestations as a result of a person's love from within. I'm not saying love is not reality. Love might just actually make reality what it is. I *am* simply saying my search for the truth about God was conducted more externally than internally—based more on physical manifestations than obscure impressions. Even though my feelings led the way at times, the end in mind was to physically observe the place they led me to. I sought physical, observable evidence—old, new, or ignored. The priority was to "see" and "touch" more than to depend on certain feelings within. This is just me.

This subjective and objective check and balance system of the human senses allows the confirmation of whether my mind accurately perceives what is actually happening, or already is. The observation of more than one person is key to verify "actual existence." I think of objective truth as a needed referee to the mind. The unchecked, subjective mind is prone to committing serious violations that can be gravely misleading, and tragically devastating to others, even to oneself. The point to understanding truth is to ultimately observe reality and achieve a peaceful unity that guides us to honor and enjoy the source of life, and that it would be sustained.

I guess if I wanted, I could think of that dream I had as reality. But if I'm honest, it's really not objective truth or reality. It was a subjective experience, and therefore, subjective truth exclusive to me—limited to me experientially. Some may assume that my dream is now manifest because others experience it through my written description, and therefore, reality. I argue this because unless I can somehow produce a great mass of rock hovering in the sky, it's not quite reality. Maybe I can, and then it would be. But someone else must be able to observe what I describe on his or her own, objectively, to make reality status; otherwise, it remains subjective, and suspect as imagined. So, in the true sense and spirit of "actual existence", I must be able to distinguish between subjective and objective truth if I am ever to truly know reality.

I figure, by holding to this standard as I search for the ultimate truth, this check and balance system will serve to help me find the deep answers about life. I feel at ease having this mindset to approach and challenge things already believed, by me, or you. Sometimes we're afraid to test the integrity of something or someone because of the potential for controversy or conflict. There should be no self-reproach in wrestling with issues when the intellect and sprit is held accountable by these guidelines when searching for truth. With respect and self-control setting the tone, everything should always be on the table of scrutiny, all meant to reach a place of solid understanding, and the ultimate truth. And for truth to be truth, it cannot contradict itself.

And so I conduct this search upon the grounds of finding the objective truth about God—existing regardless of what's in my mind or anyone's. I'm looking for reality to collide with my brain, and awaken my inner self to what's really happening—my subjective thoughts to meet the objective environment! I mean, if God is real, why should the experience of God be limited to only subjective experiences, or passing phenomena? The whole proposition of God is major. Shouldn't God be more obvious? But maybe God *does not* exist like people think, or believe?

The Hunt

One of the biggest questions I search to see answered, "Is there one truth for all people, in all places, at all times." The perception and interpretation of truth is quite precarious if not approached fairly. This quest is showing me that if truth is to even be perceived, I need to be honest and *want* to perceive it, *try* to perceive it, and learn *how* to perceive it.

I get confused when I tell myself truth is *not* something simple, but some complex, all-encompassing theory about everything in the known, and unknown universe, and why I'm here, and why you're here, and if black holes in space lead to other dimensions and times, or if ghosts and spirits visit the living, and if my beliefs and convictions have the power to create truth, what the sum of all claimed truths equals…You can just hear the matter being confounded. So for the sake of clarity, I want to keep it simple: real life is simply bound to the facts. Reality = Truth, and Truth = Reality.

The uncomplicated approach is to know the facts, and proceed to conclude and live on this basis, and, if courageous enough, to set my goals as to what is probable, not improbable. If I'm to understand and reason things of truth, I conclude that I need to both admit and realize, whether I may know *something* or not, *that* something (if it's real), exists apart from me, and my own existence, even regardless of what I believe or have faith in. From here, it is my choice to simply seek true answers and hear them. If I can remember that the *undertaking* to perceive truth is more the complex part, I can then let the facts develop the truth, and trust that the answers to my questions will be discovered. This amounts to me observing life simplistically—how truth is fact, and facts, truth. I've heard it stated that, "It only matters what you believe." In all honesty, it matters that we trust what is true. What is healthy about trusting false reality, unless reality is just one, big placebo? In part, it's easier to fantasize about reality instead of intimately engaging it. But I long to know and experience the truth. So maybe there's hope in all of this.

In general, it's difficult to identify, or even admit my particular biases and preferences, and avoid them getting in the way of my accurate perception of reality. Inevitably, part of me wants to believe certain things *to be* true, maybe like space aliens are visiting planet earth because life, other than us, exists in the universe. It must. Right? The shear fact of such evidence lacking makes this, at best, a theory, as of now anyway. But how many believe this to be true, or want it to be true? Millions? Billions? How about this: does it really matter? Should it be as much of a priority as we make it, because is it really fact? Is it myth? Helpful? Deceptive?

Perhaps something like this is deceptive, because it can consume a person to the point of fear and anxiety, or creating unhealthy obsessions. Perhaps it's helpful because it's good for space-alien product sales, also keeping the search into outer space alive, and funded. Or maybe it's even true. But could we be pouring billions of dollars into a black hole of false hope, sending signals and spacecrafts light years away into the outer limits without any hope of being answered, while all along there are so many things here on earth we actually *know* need our attention and money today. Yet, something so ambiguous gets such serious attention. I'm not saying I'm against UFO research, or funding for the space program. I just think our tax-spending priorities are sometimes strange, and desperately tragic in some respects.

Religion, spirituality, God, or atheism, possess similar qualities of uncertainty, and testimony. I am truly amazed about how many different religions and philosophies there are to follow. These pages could be filled over and over with them, covering many people over thousands of years, and roads they traveled; but it really boils down to what I will trust in anyway. To what will I invest my attention, my hope, and my life? With so many facts available to help discover reality, does this plethora of information tell the truth? To what path shall I commit? Whom shall I listen to?

I also recognize how my family is one of the strongest influences that have helped create certain biases within me, and even steer certain allegiance. Both a strong family presence, and the great lack they're of, molds us, reaching across generations. Family can have such fervent and certain desire for its children— sometimes destructive, and sometimes a heavenly blessing. At times I've felt as though there aren't many options for who I am to become, and choose only what I've been brought up with, or what now faces me. For spite, love, others, our selves, money, power, or take your pick—many reasons and external influences govern our thoughts and choices. I know they do mine. Our worldviews are shaped by all of these factors, even more than by what may actually be true.

Through all of this, through my biased experience of life, I am managing to put aside as many preconceived notions as possible, positive and negative, about what I think life is about. I'm actually beginning to hear and observe things in the deepest ways. My goal is to observe life in the freshest way possible, tuning into the very essence of reality in hopes of discovering the ultimate truth about whether God exists, and who God is.

Common Ground Facts

"Common Ground" fact number one: we all have an opinion. In light of this, I must first prepare against being misled by understanding the nature of opinion, my own opinion, and how "opinion" itself sometimes fits into the character of deception. I understand opinion as simply a view or perspective a person holds about truth or facts, or anything for that matter. A scientifically, well-linked series of opinions based on facts and assumptions can lead to theory, but still remains speculation at best. Opinion and theory cross over into the realm of truth when they are confirmed as factual or false—actual existence, or completely disproved. Until then, opinion remains a subjective point of view, and born out of guesses yet to be proven.

If God is obvious, facts and objective truth should reveal the truth about God. So how can anyone be sure of what the facts are? People are always being deceived, have always been, and will continue to be. It's when opinion, and facts, and theory, and truth get all mixed up, that the opportunity for deception and delusion ripen. When they are intentionally confused for the purpose of agenda, fraud strikes. At this point, there is a choice: to live in the knowledge of reality, or choose to be bound by a subjective state of mind, being spoon-fed snake oil, where certain and specific truths are commonly denied, and reality resisted. Ignorance resides in this place.

The perfect example is with relationships. Who hasn't had or needed warning, except the fortunate, about potential dysfunctions or dangers of a relationship we're in—sometimes valid and sometimes paranoia? But how many times might we deny this input for the sake of "love?" I would say it's almost epidemic. It's so easy, and feels so natural to only trust the subjective perspective, refusing the interruption of objective contributions. In other words, when my opinion of my companion conflicts with "actual reality", I might not care because I'm smitten. The only way for me to reconcile is to investigate and prove, or deny and hope for the best. If I choose the route of denial and hope, the question in a sense becomes, "Do I feel lucky?" It may work out to be positive, or my life could take a turn for the worst. Either way, I'm the one responsible for learning the objective truth about my circumstance. This is the way I am approaching the truth about reality. I see it as my personal responsibility to know what is true for certain.

It's not unreasonable to envision what reality is, and how I see myself in relation to it, but my vision must be based on a true form of reality, and not only my opinion, faith, or hope. Discovery is part of having vision, but is only helpful when I respect its findings. I must be fair when I find things that disturb me, and not sweep them under the rug and fabricate falsehoods or propaganda that fit what I want to believe. Referring back to the previous example, it amounts to me making wise decisions based on reality about the relationship with my companion. On the other hand, when whatever truth I might discover is rejected, whether or not sought, the opportunity to become more intimate with reality is denied. Not everything I come to hear and see is painless, and fits the paradigm I hold, or my bias, but truth is a roadmap of the past, the present, and is an aid to moving forward into the unknown future. Objective truth tests the subjective vision, and keeps me from being mindlessly lost.

Maybe some of us think we're all lost regardless of the truth, on a globe, spinning indefinitely through space with no end in sight. Maybe you're of the school of thought that life is about finding comfort in what we hope to be true—just to survive life, not rotting in despair. And all the concoctions of human beings are simply to provide the illusion of security and control so that we don't, in fact, lose our minds while we live this life. Could we handle God not existing, knowing that once we die our experience of being alive ceases? Would we be able to deal with this final answer, and still maintain the every-day life? Whichever true, the responsible and intelligent path is to know the truth about this, and then live accordingly. I must again agree with Socrates that, "The unexamined life is not worth living." Who or what is the master of our destiny? What are we trying to make of it? And so, I examine life.

My search is about finding facts, and knowing the true reality. I say give it to me! I admit, it's a difficult thing to separate my hope, bias, and preference that life will not end, and I will eternally get to experience being alive in some form. And even the notion eternity is better than the present is something I hope for. But I'm willing to see it differently. I'm open to being educated and witness the truth about this matter—even if I discover there is no eternity. So I ask, does God exist? What is my ultimate fate? What can I know for sure? Is there anything solid and concrete anywhere to help set the record straight? These are my questions. The answers must exist.

The Obvious – Ground Zero

We do have common ground. It's just a matter of identifying it. I want to work from the most obvious points and facts we know of to establishing a true perspective of reality. To start with, this may sound absurd, but "common ground" fact number two: I'm alive and breathing. I find myself, along with billions of others on a mass of matter about eight thousand miles wide, fed energy from a burning hot, fiery spherical sun a hundred times bigger, and about ninety three million miles away, give or take. We here on earth, find ourselves at a safe distance from this sun that makes ripe the growth of physical life existing around and within us, all contained in a solar system within a galaxy, surrounded by what looks to be an endless number of galaxies, made up of an immeasurable amount of stars. How old? Who *really* knows for certain? The point is that we are all here, existing. We are all in this together. This we know for sure, for a fact. There have been billions of people who came before us, and surely many more after. This is common ground everyone shares.

Our predecessors have documented many things. As a result, both clarity and confusion about our past is plentiful. Religions, philosophies, theories, and everything under the sun are on the table, set by those before us, and being set as you and I live on. How do I sort this information, these tools or distractions, into a clear interpretation of reality? The option to try certainly exists, but can this even be done? The only sure way to make sense of it all is to link the obvious.

In the face of destiny, it's also obvious I will die some day—"common ground" fact number three: death or departure from this earth is inevitable. Therefore, as a good steward *of* life, it's in everyone's best interest to survive, strive for the best quality of life, and for the longest duration. It's instinctual. What's there to lose, except the very life we have? Whether for eternity, or just for one more day, we strive to say, "I love you" to the ones who mean so much to us. Life is precious and worth more than we could ever care for it. The beat of our heart and the essence of who we are is a gateway to the apex of life itself—whatever this apex may be. Being alive and experiencing death is common ground we all share.

Through my very being, I reach for the source of vitality, yearning for more. If I'm honest with myself, I do not want my life to end, and want to combat any pain or despair that threatens my hapiness or life. I want to live. I want to experience freedom, and good things, and love others, and receive love. I sense my life is worth something valuable. This awareness is innate. It's in me whether I admit it or not. I then ask myself, how I can make my life meaningful. How can I love, and be loved? These questions and yearnings are common ground amongst human existence. And I know the primary answer depends initially on being alive, and staying alive to continue experiencing it. But precisely what does this mean: who is living, and who is dying? I've heard I am just a cosmic spec that will once again return to nothingness, but I don't sense this within me. Even still, I must remain open to the possibility of ultimate nothingness. I hope this isn't the case, and who would? If it's true, it's true though. What could I do? Wanting to be alive in one form or another is common ground for all.

God?

There are over 6.5 billion people living on this earth as of now**, and approximately eighty-five percent of us believe in God, or identify with some religion. Only fifteen percent of us are non-religious or do not believe in the existence of God***. Even if these reported instances are not perfectly accurate, I

** U.S. Census Bureau, U.S. and World Population Clocks – POPClocks, http://www. census.gov/main/www/popclock.html as of April 2005.
*** Encyclopedia Britannica Online, Article, http://www.britannica.com/eb/article?tocId= 9396555&query=religion&ct=eb, UN medium variant figures for mid-2003, as given in World Population Prospects: The 2000 Revision.

would conclude that the vast majority of us do believe in God, and have faith that a higher power exists. And just because people trust in God, or believe there is a God, doesn't make God, God. God just "is", if in fact, God exists. So what do we make of the fact that not everyone believes a God exists? This raises a multitude of questions to start. Can it be true for both, that God exists to some, and does not exist to others? Does Mike, for instance, who does not believe God exists, working side by side with God-believing Suzie, somehow live in a different reality, sharing only the reality of a job with Suzie? This concept is preposterous, and suggests one or both believe a false reality—subjective notions at best. This is where our common ground begins to dramatically fracture.

Even amongst those who do believe in God, disagreement about the very nature of God persists, to say it lightly. This lack of common ground continues fracturing humankind. Is it possible for our world to identify and unite under the *actual* reality—a reality true for all people, in all places, at all times, and live as a wholly united people? Is there one reality, or many? Should we agree to disagree, or would this approach just be avoiding the issue? The opportunity to realize the true reality exists, and doing so would dramatically affect the way we look at the world—the way we treat each other. Is this hope realistic, or idealistic? Can our actual common ground be fully realized? My search marches toward the answers to these questions.

Chapter Three

God

"Both the grand and the intimate aspects of nature
can be revealed in the expressive photograph.
Both can stir enduring affirmations and discoveries,
And can surely help the spectator in his search
for identification with the vast world
of natural beauty and the wonder surrounding him."
– Ansel Adams

So here I am in 1988, graduated high school, with this aching burden to discover the truth and the meaning of life. And even though my pursuit for the truth about God is taking shape, I'm only eighteen. For most of us teenagers, this equates to some confusion, coupled with certain insecurities, wrapped in idealistic ways of thought, and duped with the feeling like there's all the time in the world left. With high school behind me, my plan for the next six months is to continue working my job at the grocery store to save up enough money to buy a car and some snow skis in time for the first snowfall. My goal is to get to the Sierra Mountains and enjoy the coming winter. And of course, start college.

But I realize I needed a second job to get my ski gear before winter arrives. I remember my last English teacher telling me his son in-law had a painting company, and was looking for some help. So, I call, and he hires me. And now, until the rain shows up I will spend the days, when I'm not working at the grocery store, painting houses in San Francisco. Time passes quickly, and before I know it, I'm driving my car to go buy skis. Winter is here, and for the next couple of seasons, I look forward to the fresh Sierra snow.

My high school senior year ski trip to Lake Tahoe brought back memories of when my mom took my brother and me skiing as little kids. And now with the world ahead of me I want to revisit the snow-covered mountains on my own. I want to ski like I have never skied before. I want to head down the slopes that I was too little to ski before, or not good enough. Deep inside I feel my wings begin to spread! This is something I simply have to engage, to learn more of who I am. In a way, I sense this freedom leading me to a deeper meaning about life. The freedom of choice is teaching me I have some bigger choices to make—work, family, and resolving the truth about reality. But still, the search to know the truth about God is remains a choice, or a process I need committing to. Fortunately, I eventually make the commitment.

Steady Plodding

At twenty years old, I strongly sense God exists. A while back, I had a few physical encounters and sensed a spiritual presence around, or near me. It was things I acknowledged and said about God that led to these experiences. My sincere belief that God existed made the hair on my skin stand up. Tingling sensations were about my body, and I wept—overwhelmed by something seemingly outside of me that want to connect within. Still, even at that point concrete reasons lacked as to what these encounters meant and if it was just my brain producing those feelings and sensations.

As my search continues, lots of options face me about what to believe, and whom to believe. I wonder how answers I find will affect my lifestyle, but I want to *know* far more than I'm worried about changing, while simultaneously being afraid of what I might find and what it could ultimately mean. But I must do my best and remain as neutral as possible if I'm to truly to know the objective truths about reality.

Deep conversations with different people about reality are proving to be intense adventures. Their own spiritual experiences are providing diverse perspectives. This hunt for truth is exciting, and I'm very open to whatever truth I find. It's ultimately about connecting the pieces of life's puzzle. Most of the people I grew up around believe in God, and it's also becoming apparent that to most, God means church and Jesus, or religion. Part of my search is geared toward challenging the faith of those devoted to organized religion. I hold the theory that they follow the masses "just because" everyone else does. After all, it seems a real stretch believing Jesus is God, or God a prophet, or an individual telling of his internal vision about reality, but now dead and gone. It's all or nothing with these ways, and quite the leap to take to believe.

Jesus and the others are irrelevant to my encounters with God. It's God I communicate with, not them. I don't see or hear any historical icons, and the obvious conclusion seems to be that God is reachable aside from any established religion. I realize this is my opinion, and maybe I'm missing something, but one key thing fueling my search is the real, personal and spiritual encounters occurring with me. Weeks and months pass without any type of spiritual encounter, but are frequent enough to generate anticipation of them. Being able to sense the presence of God, or this *something,* draws me to exclusively trust *it* exists. How could it not? To me, this is not religion, but something real. And to where this is all leading me, I can't say. But as for now, I look at religion as being dead.

I admit that part of me is very ignorant about religion. A set of rules, an angry God, attending a church service once a week, restraining natural desires in hopes of pleasing God—this is religion, as I understand it. I know I don't really get it, but what do I make of the fact I don't want to get it? Where I'm from, most people I know who believe in God consider themselves Christian. That's just my culture, also mixed with different religions, and ideas about God, with few who would profess there is no God at all.

Others try to convince me that the spiritual presence I sense is Jesus, because that's what they believe. I am told and shown in the Bible where Jesus is recorded saying, "I am the way, the truth, and the life. No one comes to the Father, except through Me." The "Father" being, God, I'm told. This is too intolerable to deal with! How could this be the only way to God? In my opinion, they aren't convincing. I guess I could set out and verify the facts about Jesus to know for sure, but the whole idea turns me off. Instead, I am seeking God as if God has not yet been revealed. Perhaps this approach is arrogant and self-important, but I want a pure connection, avoiding preconceived notions and distractions. So not really knowing how to pinpoint the essence of God, my inner self is where I have started. My assumption: understanding what I am, and what makes my heart, beat, will reveal God. In fact, God should be at the very core in some noticeable way if God is real.

I've decided that seeking truth is the aim, and my conscience has become a key tool. Knowing and understanding how my conscience works is, in itself, a spiritual experience. It is a form of communication—if nothing else, with my own being. Some say it's simply communication with the "inner self". Slice it any way you want, to me this is communication. I just happen to think it's with God, because when I hear and follow this inner voice, things seem to work out much better than when I don't. The goodness and positive course in my life has to be God. Right? In some way, it's like a guardian watching over, and lighting the way. To my detriment, I don't always listen to its leading.

I perceive that my conscience is somehow linked to the super-natural. Acting upon the direction of my conscience provides constant, personal growth and improvement, along with certain wisdom. Can I claim ultimate credit for the source, denying God for success? Perhaps. But I'm not prepared to believe it's just me at the core. This intervention is coming from somewhere outside of me. I'm not reading many books, or under the teaching of anyone on the subject of reality. So, I conclude the knowledge and guidance is coming from somewhere beyond my subjective experience. However, my personal, subjective opinion needs corroboration.

With my conscience experience as my main tool, I consider whether or not this genuine manifestation of my conscience can be corrupted in some way? Could I intentionally or unintentionally distort this connection and become unable to hear it's leading? I'd be foolish to think jeopardy is not an actuality, and that my conscience could not become weakened, by choice or tragedy. There are too many questions. And at the sake of losing touch with God, I am following my conscience more and more. It is too great a risk to allow anything to get in the way of this positive interaction—especially me. I seek the strength and desire to know the true reality about God and life through this avenue.

The suspense continues to build. I detect the truth about the essence of life drawing closer. But how close? My twenty-first birthday has just passed, and a deep loneliness consumes my soul. Lying down, I grieve. I search my mind. "Where will I turn for comfort?" I think of the people closest to me, but ultimately realize they cannot provide the consoling I long for. I turn inward, and the weight of my despair holds my thoughts captive. I run through the options in my head and it suddenly, yet simply dawns on me. What was I thinking? "I'll turn to God!"

Not a moment later, a burst of energy seems to shoot into my feet, up through me, filling my lungs with a breath of air! I resolve that God is present, waiting to be called upon! God is walking my life with me! For the first time, God is more real than ever! And the faithfulness of this presence propels my confidence to trust that everything will work out for the rest of my life. From this moment on, I trust there is nothing to worry about, because I know God is truly with me. Our relationship becomes more real. I called upon God, and God is here—Whatever God is, Whoever God is.

Through my search I grow in strength and independence, not apart from God, but conquering my fears. Common insecurities about rejection, risk, my future, and death are diminishing. More and more my trust is now placed in God. The notion that God has a plan for my life grows. Nothing yet is specific, but a realization grows. I see the choice to seek and hope for truth and power over fear and doubt. It's becoming clear the truth will be found.

The fulfillment of and commitment to my destiny is shadowing the importance of pursuing anything else. Don't get me wrong. I do have a job. Since my days at the grocery store and painting houses, I now work in the hardwood flooring trade with my hands, committed to working hard and performing quality workmanship. I attend college courses here and there, but my passion is to know the ultimate truth about God. I'm invested to know this ultimate answer. Then, I can start living accordingly. Perhaps reckless to most, I trust my destiny in God will satisfy the best of dreams, because I am pursuing why I was created. I want my career to be the fulfillment *of* my destiny, guided by heavenly passion. And purpose is gradually revealing itself through this simple, yet enthusiastic act of seeking God. I continue to believe in God as a higher power, hungering for the precise reveal.

Even though I question the relevancy of Jesus, I want to know what the Bible says about life in general. So for the first time, I open the Bible with the desire to comprehend its message for whatever it turns out to be. Starting in Genesis, I end up in the Gospel of John, reading about the love Jesus has for God the Father. I believe I'm developing this same kind of love for God, and the realization of my connection with God brings tears. Part of me doesn't want to reject Jesus. He exudes such a pure heart, testified by others. But there just isn't enough to go on, and take that leap, trusting in who the Bible says He is. There is this nagging burden for something more than what others have simply written, or said, or even what I feel. I take the position that Jesus was a great man who just realized the potential we all have. At the same time, being honest with myself, I understand that a man isn't great if he claims to be God and isn't. It's deception, insanity, or true, but only one of these.

The main stumbling block for me is the fact that humans wrote the Bible. No one has to wonder about the nature of human beings. We can be so very deceptive, which is the root to most of my skepticism about everything. Besides, we're not just talking about some irrelevant matter—this is life and death. It matters what we trust in. Part of my struggle with the Holy Bible is my lack of desire to put forth the effort to honestly understand and study it in great depth. Instead, I yearn for something else from God—but do I even comprehend what I'm looking for? One thing is certain: forget the subjective or emotional. Let me witness something powerful and striking to settle every ounce of doubt. I search for that something that no one can deny—not even me. After all, I'm human. Imperfect. I find myself doubting even the things I thought I was sure about. Even though I strongly sense a supernatural influence, I still wonder if I'm imagining things. If I cannot maintain my sanity, what am I really gaining? I suppose I ultimately wouldn't know because I would have lost my mind. In light of this, I still have doubts. Maybe I'm being selfish, but I'm asking for something prominently obvious.

The wrestle with God persists, as does challenging the faith of the "religious", and the Bible. I am doing my best to test everything objectively. I wish I could be a better sport, but I have to know, and push limits. Part of my problem at times is *me* just wanting to be right. I admit! Who wants to be wrong? I don't set out to make unnecessary waves and occasionally offend people. Whether pride, embarrassment, or loss of control, I grapple with the possibility I am wrong about things, but which things? My wrestle with God sometimes shifts into a battle with myself to be unbiased toward knowing the truth. I find it difficult. "It doesn't matter who or what God is?" I tell myself. "Isn't the whole point to simply know, if it can be known?" Sometimes, I simply fear my own doubts and frustration finds its home in confrontation. This isn't right, I know.

The longing continues for something out of the ordinary, a powerful statement that identifies life's real meaning and framework. My heart cries out, "God, reveal the truth about who you are!" Something extremely tangible must exist—other ways aside from religion. There's got to be something else out there to put a finger on which says, "That's God!" Can you relate to this? There is so much fear and resistance in placing absolute trust in anything, let alone in God who seems so hidden. Trusting the writings of others out of the distant past is major, and just about ridiculous. How could one religion over another be the only, unchanging way? What about everyone else who doesn't believe this? There must be a way to make sense of it all.

A Valley of Decision

At the age of twenty-one, I cordially accept an invitation to take a trip to a National Park in the Sierra Mountain, a place I had never been before. And the closer and closer this trip comes, the more I hear God communicating about where I am headed. Anticipation and excitement grow. I keep sensing something is there, up in those mountains, but what? Something. What is "something?"

It's not easy to explain, but as the day of arrival comes closer, I look forward to more of the truth being revealed by God. Answers I've been wrestling for seem to be approaching. Now, my main expectation about this trip into the mountains is what God will reveal to me. This is an appointment with the truth. I sense it. I don't recall ever seeing photographs of this area, but had only heard of it.

Reputation of this world-renowned valley speaks of natural beauty and grandeur, as many trek from all around the globe to gaze upon it. But this remained a place not on my list of things to see, until now. My schedule is set to visit more of who God is, and after this trip, I will return with a great deal more understanding. Why I think this—I don't know. For now, I can't stop thinking of being there. Counting down the days, finally it's time to go.

Awaking to the dark of the morning, a new day has dawned. A certain scent makes the air in the room alive. I am refreshed by the sensation of cool air through my nose. The thought of visiting this new place has me restless. I ponder the possibilities that await me in this so-called natural paradise and the mystery that I feel I am about to embark upon.

Many hours of travel pass. Driving up into the mountains, through the forest, and down the summit, a great valley beholds itself. The valley is truly striking, possessing awesome walls of granite—the ground offering them up to the sky.

The search is on, driving through this valley, intuitively scanning the walls as if trying to read them. My eyes comb each passing face of granite. "Where is it?" I think to myself. "It." What is "it"? I still don't know. I only know I need to keep looking. And, approaching the deeper part of the valley, there *it* stands.

We meet. Walking toward the river, I stop at an old, dead tree trunk, and just gaze up at this towering mass for several minutes. I now realize I was brought into this place, to see this mountain! "*It* is there." And after my engaged stare I turn around, and go to help set up camp. My heart patiently anticipates the unfolding.

Deep inside, I am puzzled, confused, burdened, and excited all at once. I don't know what I'm looking for. I don't understand what I'm supposed to learn here. I don't even fully grasp why I sense something is waiting for me to see in this valley, if I'm even supposed to see anything. Maybe I will hear something. Maybe it will be nothing, and I'm just working myself up. But within me, I can't escape something calling me to discover a hidden truth. It's not that I hear voices, or see apparitions guiding me to another dimension. I sense the surreal and normal surround me at once. I don't feel out of place, but at the same time it seems as though I'm entering into a new element.

Finding the right words to describe what's turning inside me proves exceedingly difficult. The only thing I really know is that I am here for a specific reason—a reason I have no knowledge of. Seeing these granite walls for the first time tells me I'm standing on this valley's ground to search them for something about God. This realization becomes more and more clear with each passing hour. And my attention returns to converge upon Half Dome again and again.

The very same morning, I again walk toward the river and simply stare into the face of Half Dome. For about twenty minutes I just gaze. Nothing specific consumes my thoughts. I just seem to connect with the reason I am here. "*It* is there," I say again, as I walk away. *What* is there, I still have no idea, but whatever it is, I'm convinced it's there. One thing for sure, the power of God drew me here to resolve my uncertainties.

By dusk of the next day, sitting at the table at our campsite, out underneath the colossal presence of Half Dome, my place by the river invites me. So I go, staring to penetrate the mystery this great monolith holds.

This mass of granite towering in the sky is like a magnet, pulling at my heart. I can't seem to break away. Looking up, waiting, anticipating, I peer into this giant wall of stone. Barriers within my mind begin to part, as images emerge with stark contrast.

I begin to perceive the shape of a head. My eyes fix on its nose, eye, mouth, as its horn begins to show. I see the head of a beast! Its horn outlines the very ridge of Half Dome! Shock, and a sense of fear come over me!

"What in the world is this?!!!" Tears of revelation fall from my eyes over the super-natural nature of what I behold. I look back again, almost in disbelief. "Is this really there?" My second glance solidifies the image even more. I recompose, dry my face, and look up. "God, this is amazing! I can't believe my eyes!"

Who is this beast I see on the wall? What does this image represent? It makes me think of Satan. Time begins standing still as I stare into this massive image, swept away in wonder of this picture I witness.

Image of the Beast

This animal-like appearance dominates the west side of this great stone, wall. Black streaks of granite make up its mane, the trees its hair. Its body shoots out into the mountainside, resting its wing below, as if stalking prey!

The ancient texts depicting a similar image is found in the Holy Bible. It says, "the devil, prowls around like a roaring lion, seeking someone to devour" (1 Peter 5:8), and "...disguises himself as an angel of light" (2 Corinthians 11:14).

What kind of angel is this, who masquerades as enlightenment? The previous picture showed both the beast crouched down as if ready to pounce, also having a wing as its limb. Satan is described as being "...fallen from heaven..." according to Isaiah 14:12, and is "...the prince of the power of the air..." (Ephesians 2:2). Satan is also depicted as "...roaming about on the earth and walking around on it" (Job 2:2). I'm seeing the relation between how the Bible describes the devil and the images on this mountain.

One of the most amazing aspects of this beastly image is actually what cannot be seen from the valley's most common views. Looking at Half Dome from the floor of Yosemite Valley, I realize the beast is concealing its true intention behind its shoulder. The Book of Revelation refers to the beast as "...the great dragon...the serpent of old who is called the Devil and Satan, who deceives the whole world" (Revelation 12:9). It's only from a different vantage point am I able to discern the full character of this beast upon this wall. Rising high above the valley to the northeast I look down.**** Remarkably a more complex beast presents itself, growling, mouth open and saliva dripping from its upper lip. I see its teeth, gnashing and looking ready to devour as the Bible describes. This fleshy snarl cannot be missed!

This image is so apparent from this angle and in this light that it almost needs no pointing out. I've seen Half Dome from this angle in full light before the sun goes down, and its full image is not nearly as apparent as when the darkness begins rides up its face as the sun sets. This time of day is most optimal to see the snarl of the beast as the light cuts across the massive face of Half Dome. All this is taking place and witnessed from high above, yet from the valley floor you would never know—it is somehow disguised.

Its lips curl around razor-like incisors waiting to strike. The jaw-line and crinkled nose, along with the creases of its face display intense hostility and aggression. The neckline rides up the backside of the mountain, connecting the body and creature-like skull with its thick and powerful neck muscle.

I can't even really find the right words to describe these features. The shape of the head is frightfully eerie, sending a chill through me. I'm not sure I
**** 　　Photo opposite page © 2007 Eu-Jin Goh, All Rights Reserved.

even fully comprehend its composition. All I know, this is like some beast out of a motion picture that is yet to be made, but already manifested according to this mountain. The face seems multi-faceted, with two noses, and two mouths—almost two heads in one. I could go on, but this image paints more words than I can begin to think of.

What does this mean? Why is this there? And even as intense as this is for me, I still feel as though I'm missing a major part of what I came to witness, here on Half Dome. This mountain is not yet done with me. I sense God has more in store to draw from as another day passes.

Image of a Man

I walk toward the river to catch my breath. Again, tears. The sensation of an awesome presence is enveloping me. I am drawn to look deeper into Half Dome and see a human-like appearance, but jagged and wrathful. The most distinct feature being a great shout! I'm not able to pinpoint who this is, but the glory speaks wonderment!

"Who is this? Whose face is before me?" I don't know why, but I think of Jesus. It's nothing like I'd think Jesus would look. How could I anyway? But why I think of Him I don't know. I just do.

My endless gaze also identifies a very human portrait, separate from the jagged image—a whole, new image. His right profile is made out, along with his nose, and cheekbone

His hair flows down under a shadowy beard-like jaw line, and the detail of the white of his eye is stark, staring sternly into the beast that is opposite. This person also bears a jagged looking headpiece resting on top of his head. And from this side profile, I even see this face transforming into a second image.

He looks just slightly outward to His right. His eye begins to widen, and His mouth opens. His face starts becoming distorted, and less human-like. Another face seems to rise up from below, moving into the large, jagged and wrathful image sharing the same shout—the one of him I first noticed. Could this really be Jesus?

"Pilate then took Jesus and scourged Him. And the soldiers twisted together a crown of thorns and put it on His head…" (John 19:1-2). "…Jesus took with Him Peter and James and John His brother, and led them up on a high mountain by themselves. And He was transfigured before them…" (Matthew 17:1-2).

The Book of Revelation says, "His eyes *are* a flame of fire, and on His head are many diadems", or crowns (Revelation 19:12). And the shout! This image is clearly letting loose a massive shout. The Bible says, "Listen closely to the thunder of His voice, And the rumbling that goes out from His mouth. Under the whole

heaven He lets it loose, And His lightning to the ends of the earth. After it, a voice roars; He thunders with His majestic voice, And He does not restrain the lightnings when His voice is heard. God thunders with His voice wondrously, Doing great things which we cannot comprehend" (Job 37:2-5).

This is more than amazing! The deeper I look into the images upon Half Dome, the more the Bible tells of them. I can't deny the accumulation of descriptions: the twisted crown, the transfiguration, an appearance as lightening, eyes like a flame of fire, and a mighty shout! Could this be the image of God?

I know I don't hear the shout. I only see it. It's a picture of One shouting, captured in time, frozen. I see an illustration of fury that makes me think of things I've heard about, stories of God judging humankind, angry with wrath at the end of the world. Could this be God's way of saying that He is Jesus—through Half Dome, and through the Bible? The case for this image on Half Dome being Jesus is mounting.

And even where the Book of Revelation says, "Then I looked, and behold…one like a Son of Man, having a golden crown on His head…" (Revelation 14:14), at sunset, the face of Half Dome lights up, and the twisted crown becomes a "glowing, yellowish crown" upon His head!

This is truly amazing! I begin to think, "How is this not a sign from God? How could this not be Christ?" I can't think of anyone else who fits these images on Half Dome more than Jesus. No one! I'm having trouble believing it's *not* Jesus. And then, I'm constantly brought back to the fact God has put this in Yosemite Valley. Of all places—on Half Dome! It's not like some secret mountain in some remote wilderness no one knows about. On the contrary, this is front and center. For all we know, these images have existed on this massive wall an eternity before Jesus even walked this earth! How could I not be convinced the supernatural is pointing to Jesus? This is no mere coincidence. This has got to be God!

Each aspect of the images on Half Dome, alone is unremarkable. Each accruing feature is making the case for Jesus being the Man Half Dome, who is opposing the beast Satan. The face of Half Dome is shared by the snarl and teeth of a beast having a horn and wing, shared with a Man wearing a thorny crown who displays a transfiguring into a jagged appearance, as lightening perhaps, and eyes like a flame of fire. At sunset the Man has a golden crown that appears in the place of the thorny one. He has a mighty shout. All of these features are concentrated onto the face of Half Dome—landmark to a world-renowned destination; revealed to me at the point in time my soul searches intensely for the truth about God. It's not about just one or two isolated aspects, but everything together marking this as

supernatural. This whole, big picture indicates a divine signature. Just thinking about why and how these images are on Half Dome is mystifying and intriguing. Even right now, multiple web cams are aimed at the face of Half Dome accessed at www.yosemite.org! Why? For the simple reason that even without the knowledge of these images, there is something awesome and powerful about this magnificent mountain crying out to be witnessed.

This sign sits amidst a forest of granite in this great valley cut by once present, and ominous glaciers. These glaciers occupied its depths to one day recede, cutting and carving steep walls of stone revealing genuine raw beauty, awesome to behold. A dome of granite resting deep in the valley awakes to be engraved by the hand of God with a chisel of ice. Sweeping glaciers slice away this rock's face displaying a magnificent force, guided by the hand of God. A might so physically powerful, a mound of hardened magma was transformed into a sculpted half dome of art—the stone itself now displaying a supernatural message. Only God could create such a work by ripping the face of a stone mountain with a passing sea of ice. Only God is capable of secretly carving a formation in the sky without anyone knowing until the moment God chooses it to be witnessed.

The best explanation for these images upon this wall is that this beast is Satan, and Half Dome remarkably bears witness of Jesus! Many of us know of Yosemite Valley, of the Sierra Mountains in California. Its awe-inspiring character unsurprisingly captures the hearts of so many, who may have always sensed something peculiar, but couldn't quite name their feelings. I gather this hidden message upon Half Dome will help confirm people's deeper stirrings about this place. Those who've experienced the beautiful aspects of Yosemite know them well—wondrous landscapes hosting magnificent vivid blooms; blooms who push up anew through the melting snow that in turn feed the rushing rivers pouring from the sky. Half Dome stands peering out across this landscape, almost as the guardian. Its shape is unforgettable, unlike anything other, possessing subtle mystique. The atmosphere in Yosemite Valley is heavenly and humbling, amassing an international multitude, who come attempting to capture this boundless, true wonder. And of the millions who've gazed upon Half Dome, how many have seen only mountains of odd-shaped stone, looking past this deeper meaning? Perhaps we've all viewed life this way, seeing intimidating mountains of meaningless features representing a void between God and us. And whether observing nature or pondering our personal lives, finding purpose seems even more distant. But I'm finding it doesn't have to be this way.

God is communicating through this instrument of Half Dome. I don't fully know the whole story yet, but it's something grand. At the same time I realize this natural amazement is ultimately *just* a mountain. And without God this granite face is not fully alive. I also now recognize the Bible as playing a critical role to knowing the truth about these images, and life itself. I sense God is not calling myself, or anyone to make an idol of worship out of Half Dome, or even the images upon it. I *am* gathering that attention is being called to God, to understand this message and what it means to our lives. There is no need, calling, desire, or whatever word you choose, to fall on my knees, and bow to worship this sign. The Bible even declares, "Let no one keep defrauding you of your prize by delighting in self-abasement and the worship of the angels, taking his stand on *visions* he has seen, inflated without cause by his fleshly mind" (Colossians 2:18). I am finding that only God is to be worshipped. I want to keep this sign in perspective.

I can only conclude that this sign simply, yet profoundly declares God is real and in our midst. We behold the image of Christ, recorded by God on a tablet of stone that reaches the sky, able to be seen by millions from around the globe—through pictures already existing that cover the globe, and cameras fixed upon it. I don't know why it has gone unseen all this time but I trust God has a plan. What matters now is this dormant sign sleeps no longer.

I am fully committed to hearing what God is saying through this message upon Half Dome, and to learn what I am to be doing with my life. Even though my questions have increased, I know they will be answered. My soul is being settled. The ultimate truth is unraveling before my very eyes. The sign on this giant granite wall, in this impressive valley is not meant to remain hibernating in the wilderness. And now, an aching burden to learn of what it's saying becomes my mission. I trust by understanding this message, God will be understood, and the only way to understand, is to know more *of* God. What's the next step?

Chapter Four

The Battle

"There is no neutral ground in the universe;
every square inch, every split second,
is claimed by God and counter-claimed by Satan."
– C.S. Lewis.

Inside I'm wrestling to understand why some of us saw the epic mass of rock hovering in the sky, woven with streams of cloud, when others did not. I go on to ask another, and another, "What about you? You're shaking your head no! How is it we're all standing here, yet you don't have an answer as to why you didn't see this thing in the sky right above your head just minutes ago?"

I'm confounded. Out of the fifteen or so people standing here, some amazingly did not see this sight! I get the notion, it's not likely they missed it because it happened too fast, or they just came late to the scene. They were here the whole time, yet blinded for some reason. Simultaneously, those of us who watched and witnessed this radical event agree it happened. "Go and tell others," I say to the ones that saw.

I turn around and look back into the sky but nothing has changed—the great stone is still out of sight. I turn back to the people standing around, but they're gone. From the hill I'm standing on, off in the distance to the north, I see vast neighborhoods. Houses and houses make up the backdrop, but I see no people. No one else is around and the daylight fades to dusk.

Across the hill in the other direction there is an old looking house. I walk toward this all-wood, weathered structure. I look back down the hill to the neighborhood. A scattered multitude now moves about going in and out of the houses spread across the landscape. I keep walking toward the old house. The water-stained wood shingles tell me this small house has been here a while. But stepping onto the porch, it feels solid. Now inside the house, I look around. There is some furniture and other things, but catching my attention is the westward view of the ocean through the large window.

A slight red tint now dominates the sky, reflecting its glow over the terrain. The sea is rising and the swells are picking up. But the swells aren't coming toward the shore. They are advancing from south to north and I can see in between the rolls and rolls of swells. They aren't breaking, just flowing along, one after another. A knock at the door gets my attention. So I go to open it.

This is more of that same dream I started off describing at the very beginning of this book. It was the one that came about two weeks after my first encounter in Yosemite Valley after the images on Half Dome had been revealed to me. In part, this dream is telling me that some *see*, while some don't or won't. By seeing I mean seeing reality, seeing personal circumstances more clearly, and even seeing these images upon Half Dome. I don't fully understand why I experience spiritual blindness at times, and why suddenly I see something for the first time, which has been in front of my face or mind the whole time. Is this God allowing my sight and awareness? What is my own role in this? I want to be one who sees reality—as much as God allows me to see and as much as I can bear. But do I really comprehend what I'm asking here?

Identifying the Terrain

The dust is settling from my life-changing encounter at the foot of the infamous granite wall. My trip to the high country proved to be a full experience, but the main theme was witnessing these images on Half Dome. All the way home, I pondered the event. It's been over a month since I was there. I've asked others close to me if they too see these images, and they do. It's clear that this sign is observable to more than just me, but to anyone willing or capable of looking. So clearly they are there, these images of Christ and the beast. And *because* they are I have to learn more of who they are. I know what I've heard about Jesus and the beast, but the time has come for me to go to the Bible first hand, and read to find out more. I must continue grappling with what this sculpted message means. Is it just speaking to me or also intended for our world?

I want to better understand the great confrontation between Jesus and the beast displayed on the wall. I want the answer to the question of who Jesus really is. Where do I, or *we* fit in to all of this? It seems this sign from God is forming a common ground by establishing common evidence. I conclude upon my return from my Yosemite-encounter that since the Holy Bible most closely describes these images I see upon Half Dome, it has to be the place of further examination.

I'm compelled to continue digging for answers as my subjective experience becomes more and more real. The Bible and this sign together are revealing objective truth about God. I feel as though my inner spirit is melding with the authentic reality unveiled before my very eyes. I am inspired to go deeper and look closer at life, purpose, and for the treasure of truth. It's clear that meaning exists in order for growth, and profound understanding can be attained. I am all the more interested in learning how much more these images on Half Dome are connected to the Holy Bible. How deep does the validity of this sacred book run? From here the quest leads through the Christian scriptures in search of deeper clarity. I have a feeling I'm really going to need my learning cap for this one. Just how deep will my study take me into the reality at hand? I hope I don't get stuck here. After all, scholars spend lifetimes trying to make sense of the Biblical writings and their meanings. Who am I but a simple person trying to make clear sense of what God is revealing to me in this day. This next step is sure to be one of the heaviest workouts I've yet experienced. I continue on by taking a much closer look at the Bible.

There are many translations of the Holy Bible available. So many, I wasn't sure which version I needed to read. After vigilant research, I realized I was looking for the most accurate, up to date, word for word translation from the original language of that day into the English I'm familiar with. The New American Standard Bible by The Lockman Foundation © 1995 seems to be what I'm looking for. The purpose of their Editorial Board in making this translation was to adhere as closely as possible to the original languages of the Holy Scriptures, and to make the translation in a fluent and readable style according to current English usage[5]. I wish I could go back in time, know the languages being spoken, and comprehend all that was said first hand. But I trust there are other ways to confirm the events and people of the Bible—who they were, what they said or wrote, and what they literally meant.

Half Dome displays a great confrontation between Jesus and the beast. The image is undeniable! Where did this battle between them start? A prophet from thousands of years ago touches on the character of Satan:

"How you have fallen from heaven, O star of the morning, son of the dawn! You have been cut down to earth, You who have weakened the nations!…you said in your heart, 'I will ascend to heaven; I will raise my throne above the stars of God…I will ascend above the heights of the clouds; I will make myself like the most high'" (Isaiah 14:12-14).

This passage describes the fuel of pride that powered the spirit of Satan to want to be greater than God—to desire God's position. It is written that Jesus witnessed "…Satan fall from heaven like lightning" (Luke 10:18). The book of Revelation says, "…the great dragon was thrown down, the serpent of old who is called the devil and Satan, who deceives the whole world; he was thrown down to the earth, and his angels were thrown down with him" (Revelation 12:9).

Chapter three of Genesis accounts how the serpent tempted Adam and Eve to disobey God. They gave into the temptation and sinned. This event represents the notorious fall of humankind. And this blow of Satan to God's newest creation appears to mar mankind in the most extreme way—death. According to the Book of Genesis, this is the point in time when the death of human beings manifested itself. It's hard to imagine that before this, death was not a reality. In Genesis, God, articulated by Moses, is recalled proclaiming to Satan, "…I will put enmity Between you and the woman…He shall bruise you on the head, And you shall bruise Him on the heel" (Genesis 3:15). For the word "enmity" my Bible references Revelation 12:17: "So the dragon was enraged…and went off to make war with [those] who keep the commandments of God and hold to the testimony of Jesus…" The prophecy of Genesis 3:15 indicates that Jesus is the "enmity", or antagonist between Satan and humankind. Interestingly Moses writes of this rivalry between Jesus and Satan about 1,400 years B.C. (before Christ) was even born.

Fast-forwarding to the time of Christ, Herod the King is ruling the territory where Jesus is about to be born. He was a Roman authority over the region of Judea where Bethlehem was—where Jesus is born. King Herod heard of Jesus' birth from the group of "wise men" who were being led by a "star" to Bethlehem to honor Jesus. The Book of Matthew tells me that Herod was aware of the prophecies about the coming messiah who would be "...King of the Jews..." He concludes that the wise men are speaking of the messiah who would be this king. (Matthew 2:2). Therefore, feeling his power threatened, Herod the Great "...sent and slew all the male children who were in Bethlehem and all its vicinity, from two years old and under..." (Matthew 2:16). This documents the first tangible strike of Satan, through Herod, at Jesus when he set out to murder the baby Jesus. As a result, the Bible records that the male babies in the region he thought Jesus to be were murdered. By Herod's command death is brought on. I see a spiritual war manifested in human bloodshed. But I find that, "...an angel..." guided Jesus' parents to "...flee..." with Jesus (Matthew 2:13), and escaping death, Jesus grew to become a man despite this attempt on his life.

Luke's Gospel records how decades later Jesus and Satan meet in the wilderness. "And [Satan] led Him up and showed Him all the kingdoms of the world in a moment of time. And the devil said to Him, 'I will give You all this domain and its glory; for it has been handed over to me, and I give it to whomever I wish. Therefore if You worship before me, it shall all be Yours.' Jesus answered him, 'It is written, You shall worship the Lord your God and serve Him only'...When the devil had finished every temptation, he left Him until an opportune time" (Luke 4:5-8, 13). Jesus succeeds in resisting the devil's temptations.

In light of these events described, spanning thousands of years, I gather that Satan gained dominion of the earth the moment Adam and Eve sinned—through their disobedience to God. Before they sinned the Bible states, "God created man in His own image, in the image of God He created him; male and female He created them. God blessed them; and God said to them, 'Be fruitful and multiply, and fill the earth, and subdue it; and rule...'" (Genesis 1:27-28). Thus when Satan tempted Jesus, Satan spoke with authority over the earth. Now that Jesus has come to take back dominion Satan must feel threatened.

Jesus summed up His mission this way: "For even the Son of Man did not come to be served, but to serve, and to give His life a ransom for many" (Mark

10:45). But what does this mean—His life a ransom? The study notes in my Bible refer to Jesus as having to endure a suffering resulting in death to rescue us from sin. I'm directed to the Book of Isaiah, where it's written that, "He was pierced through for our transgressions…and by His scourging we are healed" (Isaiah 53:5). The study notes for this verse speak of forgiveness, and refer to 1 Peter 2:24 where I read, "[Jesus] Himself bore our sins in His body on the cross…" According to the Bible, Jesus was here to sacrifice Himself, foreshadowed by the Old Testament and the Pentateuch, recorded in the New Testament. He was on earth to redeem humankind from the death sin brought about.

I wondered, "how will Satan try to stop Jesus from reclaiming what Satan has—the soul of humankind?" The Bible accounts an opportune time for another strike of Satan at Jesus:

"…Satan entered into Judas… And he went away and discussed with the chief priests and officers how he might betray [Jesus] to them… behold, a crowd *came*, and the one called Judas, one of the twelve, was preceding them; and he approached Jesus… Having arrested Him, they led Him *away*… When they came to the place called The Skull, there they crucified Him and the criminals, one on the right and the other on the left" (Luke 22:3-4, 47, 54, 23:33).

And not only was Jesus crucified, I read he was physically beaten to a pulp beforehand. The Gospel of Matthew accounts, "…they spat in His face and beat Him with their fists…" (Matthew 26:67). The Gospel of Mark reads, "Some began to spit at Him, and to blindfold Him, and to beat Him with their fists, and to say to Him, 'Prophesy!'" (Mark 14:65). The Gospel of Luke says, "…the men who were holding Jesus in custody were mocking Him and beating Him, and they blindfolded Him and were asking Him, 'Prophesy, who is the one who hit You?'" (Luke 22:63-64). The prophecy they referred to was from Isaiah more than 700 years ago: "…So His appearance was marred more than any man" (Isaiah 52:14).

In 2004, the movie "The Passion of the Christ" depicted a wicked pounding and torment unleashed by the Roman soldiers who were known as having conceivably the most brutal army in ancient history. Perhaps it was not as bad as this movie portrayed, but possibly worse. Tens of millions of us saw this film, and were disturbed. Who wouldn't be? The Roman soldiers were experts in torturing human beings with evil tools. I can only deduce that they undoubtedly treated Jesus with the utmost Roman cruelty. I see Satan, through the malicious spirit of Roman warriors, unleashing his rage and rebellion upon Jesus, crowning this violent assault by crucifying Him. When I look back to the image on Half Dome of Jesus and the beast facing off, I see the parallel between the spiritual warfare depicted in the Bible and on the granite wall—both being manifested into our physical reality.

And now, "[Jesus] was…dead…" (John 19:33). It's disturbing at the very least to imagine Satan possessing the body of a man in order to help capture Jesus and bring about His death. Genesis said that Satan would "…bruise him on the heel" (Genesis 3:15). Biblical scholars attribute the "Him" in this verse to Jesus, and assign His brutal crucifixion as the "bruise" on Jesus' heel. So what then is the bruise on Satan's head? I find a verse in the Book of Hebrews saying, "…that through death He might render powerless him who had the power of death, that is, the devil" (Hebrews 2:14). This is referring to the death of Jesus that rendered the devil powerless. Yet because "…[Jesus] has risen from the dead…" (Matthew 28:7), the bruise on the head of Satan is the bodily resurrection of Jesus.

The crucifixion of Jesus and His death upon the cross made way for His resurrection, ultimately marking the point in time when God justly reclaimed His authority in the earth realm. Satan saw to it that Christ was nailed to a Roman cross. The beast hung Him to die. But Jesus was not bound by death and now the table has turned. Jesus spoke to His disciples sometime after His resurrection, saying, "…All authority has been given to Me in heaven and on earth" (Matthew 28:18). According to what is written in the Bible, Jesus is the one who now has dominion of earth, even heaven. According to the Bible, Satan's days are numbered: "…Woe to the earth and the sea, because the devil has come down to you, knowing that he has only a short time" (Revelation 12:12). Yet the earth still rages.

If Jesus is so real then...

While much of this makes sense, at the very same time I'm puzzled the way reality is set up. I mean, since God is so real, and Jesus so significant, then why does everything seem like a riddle? Why must reality be pieced together through books of antiquity, intense searches, and extraordinary occurrences instead of outright experiencing God in person? You would think, at least I do, things should be much more apparent at face value to understand and observe, instead of trying to solve a mystery. And even when I get answers it can be a struggle to comprehend them.

Even aside from Jesus, some of what God does or allows seems contradictory. If anything is possible with God, why does God let evil exist? Why would God, who has the power to do anything, allow negative and tragic circumstances? How could a loving God condemn a life to eternal torture? "Why, God, are these Your ways?"

When I fast-forward about ten years in my own life, my Gramma has passed away. She was very close to me and helped raise my brothers and me. She was so near and dear to my heart that I felt the pain as her earthly presence ripped away from my soul. For the first time, I desperately look forward to seeing someone in heaven who I had once loved on earth. My Gramma loved God and trusted in Jesus. And as I try to comprehend how I will be able to see her again, I strain to imagine. My mind keeps telling me, "It's too good to be true." What does she look like and what is she doing? It's hard to believe I will truly see her again when I die. What is everyone else in heaven doing at this very moment? I try, but can't seem to comprehend this reality. But then I stop to remind myself that God is real, heaven also. Though even in light of *this* I can't seem to comprehend it. I know God is real because Half Dome and the Bible are both physical evidences given by God. I also sense the presence of His Spirit.

To help this heavenly reality sink in I go back to the fact that I am here, on earth, existing in a physical body. I recognize that God created the earth and all life regardless of the fact I still don't fathom why or how. I mean really, how exactly did everything come into being—something from nothing? It's apparent that God created the universe, but what would it have looked like from a spectator's point of view? Nonetheless, the human body exists and works in amazing ways. And what about the female anatomy? A woman's body plays the main role of producing new life, yet I have no idea how her body got to be this way, *and* I'm innately captivated by her entire being! So with some assistance from the man, miraculously a new person is birthed through a woman. And to think, not one of us here came even close to consciously designing the human body and all its capabilities. It's truly more than amazing! Yet not knowing exactly how we exist, we still do. My observation tells me that just because I don't comprehend certain things, they still function and do in fact exist. And by realizing objective truth is available, unseen truth can be recognized—maybe not entirely, but at least in part.

So if I know something truthfully exists, but uncertain as to how it's possible, it doesn't mean "that something" equals non-existence. It just means I don't have the architectural plans in hand to fully figure it out. I can still walk into a building, take the elevator to the hundredth floor, and be on top of a city in minutes, all without technically understanding how its structure fits together and functions. Others have put it together for me to operate. And so I walk with God and anticipate eternal life. I may not fully grasp the reality of eternal life, but I am getting the impression that by understanding more of who Jesus is, I will understand as much as I am able to about eternity.

In trying to make sense about the way reality has been set in motion I understand God's ways to be expressed this way:

"'For My thoughts are not your thoughts, Nor are your ways My ways', declares the LORD. 'For *as* the heavens are higher than the earth, So are My ways higher than your ways And My thoughts higher than your thoughts" (Isaiah 55:8-9).

I can question God, challenge God, and even disagree with God. The fact remains—I am not in control over God. I merely participate on the stage of life together with others, subject to its parameters. God sets the way of all life. We just operate within it. And when it comes to evil, perhaps our ability to choose is the culprit to its existence. Perhaps injustice and suffering come out of our own mistakes—not God. But the math to being perfectly programmed by God may equal "non-life" in the fullest sense. Maybe "real-life experience" means God downloaded "free will" software into our DNA and created the intellect, constraining our choices to real consequences in order that we grow. What if God allows bad things because absolute integrity is the lifeblood of total existence? This would make sense why a consequence follows each action. So maybe Jesus has something to do with God changing an outcome that integrity is not authorized to.

When it comes to knowing how the essence of life functions, I truly have no clue. Therefore, how can I know for sure what is best for life itself more than God does? If I argue God is ridiculous for certain existing circumstances I dare to declare I know better than God, who is infinitely wiser than I. Unless I am in God's position (infinitely unlikely however), how could I ever accurately know what is truly best for the existence of all life. That kind of perspective would provide immeasurable insight.

So instead of kicking against this system God has set in place I have the opportunity to understand it, learn from it, and gain wisdom to be successful within it. The choices remain: accept the system set forth by God and grow through it; or rebel because I think God is wrong, living resentfully; or live by my own tenets just because I want to. But unless my ways overpower God's, I'm still subject to the principles and physics God already set in motion.

It's somewhat difficult to sense or perceive the real presence of God in this world with all the evil and suffering. But if God were to fully remove His Spirit from this world, perhaps terrible chaos would suddenly break loose. And maybe that's what the end of the world is all about: God removing His presence from the earth once and for all. The best I can do is keep searching the great depths of God. I reason that my efforts are best spent working to comprehend that which can be known instead of believing I can somehow change reality, or even ignore it. And God showing me Jesus is a reality. I must therefore comprehend why.

Who is Jesus?

Learning about the confrontational events that took place between Jesus and Satan helps me with the "why" on Half Dome—why they face off with such fury. But the question of "who" remains—who exactly is Jesus? My mind continuously returns to logically process the images I see on the face of Half Dome. I begin to conclude that these images combined with certain events occurring in my life, can only be supernatural. With each passing day, it becomes more and more evident that God created this amazing portrait on this monolith. I read in the Bible that, "For since the creation of the world His invisible attributes, His eternal power and divine nature, have been clearly seen, being understood through what has been made, so that they are without excuse" (Romans 1:20). The very first words of the Bible itself, in the Book of Genesis are, "In the beginning God created the heavens and the earth." There is no doubt these images are on this mountain. People did not put them there. The only real explanation is that God did.

At first I thought I was losing my mind, but the more I examined this wall I began piecing the evidence together. I realized Yosemite is one of the most visited places on earth. These images happen to be on the most unique mountain in this valley, whose face was torn asunder by ancient ice. I was searching for the deepest answers and was summoned by God to see this wonder—a wonder that is very precise in character. I see no coincidence here. At this point, I'd be unwise to think it's just a twist of fate or some great fluke. Instead, I am compelled to play this out to its logical conclusion. So I ask, "who exactly is this Jesus upon Half Dome?" The following is what I found.

Jesus said, "If I *alone* testify about Myself, My testimony is not true. There is another who testifies of Me, and I know that the testimony which He gives about Me is true" (John 5:31-32). From Jesus' point of view, He is telling us the Father, God, testifies of Jesus, and His (God's) testimony is true. From the valley floor point of view God created this spectacle I am able to observe. Half Dome testifies to the image of a man matching various descriptions from the Bible fitting Jesus, opposing a beast-like creature known as Satan. According to this line of logic, God reveals Jesus.

The most radical aspect of Jesus I discovered in the Bible is that He claimed to be God. He said, "…Truly, truly, I say to you, before Abraham was born, I am" (John 8:58). This statement made by Jesus reaches centuries back to Moses' encounters with God on the mountain with the burning bush, the Ten Commandments, and audible conversations with Almighty God. On one account, Moses was in the presence of God, and later wrote about it: "…Moses said to God, 'Behold, I am going to the sons of Israel, and I will say to them, 'The God of your fathers has sent me to you.' Now they may say to me, 'What is His name?' What shall I say to them?' God said to Moses, 'I AM WHO I AM'; and He said, 'Thus you shall say to the sons of Israel, 'I AM has sent me to you.' God, furthermore, said to Moses, 'Thus you shall say to the sons of Israel, 'The LORD, the God of your fathers, the God of Abraham, the God of Isaac, and the God of Jacob, has sent me to you.' This is my name forever, and this is My memorial-name to all generations" (Exodus 3:13-15).

In John 8:58 Jesus claims to be the "I AM" who spoke audibly to Moses, the voice being "God's." And now, thousands of years later from the time of Moses Jesus is saying He existed as the great I AM! Clearly, Jesus is saying He is God here. And His statement and claim infuriated certain Jewish leaders. They *knew* that Jesus was claiming to be God—blasphemy in their minds! And there was no way *their* God was this Jesus of Nazareth! But, according to Jesus Himself, Jesus is God.

This is major! But even major doesn't begin to describe the implications of this. Jesus did not set Himself as a great prophet, or a wise teacher, or even a man who knew God better than anyone. Jesus is saying that He *is* God. Based on my experience, the evidence for Jesus being God lays itself out this way:

- To start with, I have life. This alone is miraculous.
- I also have an internal burden to personally seek out the truth about my existence and God's, or am called by God to do so.
- I eventually come to the images upon Half Dome portraying a man and a beast—the man transforms into a face of wrath possessing a shout; the beast with a gruesome snarl; and both furiously facing off toward one another. All

this concentrated onto a famous granite wall pointing to God as the creator of it—not humans. This also happens to be a wall millions and millions have looked upon for decades upon decades, yet have not seen until now. This alone is amazing. Therefore, the creator of these images upon Half Dome is either God or some fluke of nature. If the evidence stopped here, then a fluke of nature would be a reasonable explanation, but the evidence keeps mounting so I'm going with God.

- It's true that while both a man and a beast are revealed upon Half Dome, where is the corroborating description pointing to God as having the appearance of *this* beast upon *this* wall? However, I do find corroborating, authoritative evidence that reveal God incarnate as Jesus, a description of God as having wrath and a mighty shout throughout many parts of the Bible, and even an occasion where Jesus' face was transfigured into a Godly image.

- Because Jesus fits the description on Half Dome more than anyone in history, the Bible becomes the key part of the evidence pointing to God as the One who inspired both.

- Moses claims the Ten Commandments were actually, physically inscribed by God onto stone tablets. The first and second commandments say, "You shall have no other gods before Me. You shall not make for yourself an idol, or any likeness of what is in heaven above or on the earth beneath or in the water under the earth. You shall not worship them or serve them; for I, the LORD your God, am a jealous God…" (Exodus 20:3-5). These two commandments convey that the God Moses had a relationship with doesn't want people to revere anything above God Himself.

- Jesus Himself claims to be the God who also commands no one is to worship anything other than the Father in Heaven, as God. Jesus claims to be the Great I AM of the Old Testament.

- A God-created sign just happens to give a picture of Jesus and a beast, both found in this same Bible—Jesus recorded as being God, the beast recorded as being the devil.

- And because Jesus is present as a Man transforming into One having the mighty shout on Half dome, I take it as God saying "This is who I AM." Since God created Half Dome, why would God reveal someone else who claims to be God if they are in fact not?

- I must therefore conclude that Jesus has got to be God according to this evidence.

My conclusion would look something like this:

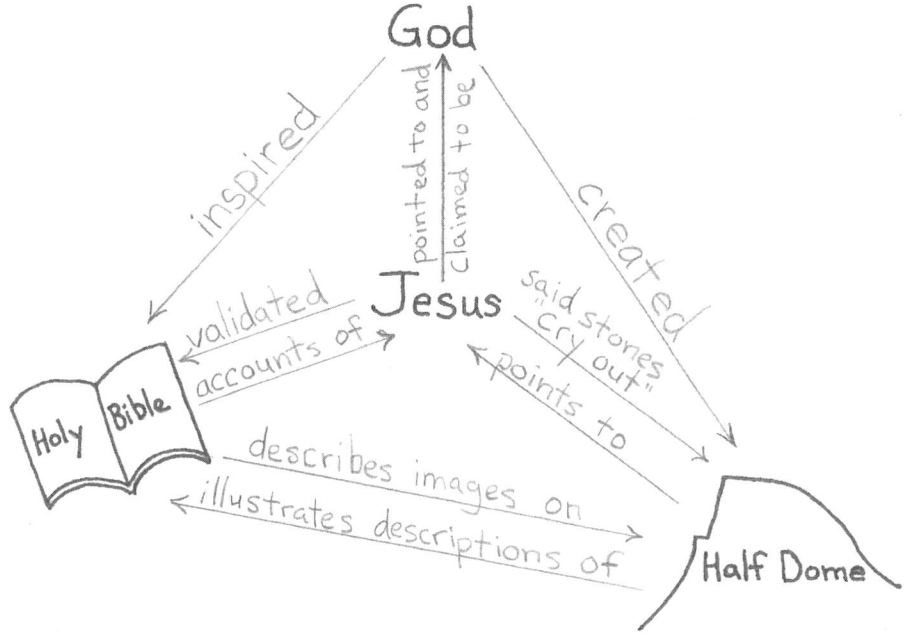

Again, the only individual other than Jesus being revealed on Half Dome is the beast, which according to the Bible is understood to be God's main adversary. What other individual or creature in our known world history fits the description and situation more than Jesus and the evil beast? I don't have another answer other than the one being laid out here. It is far more difficult for me to trust that the images upon Half Dome are some freak of nature—an accident, a coincident, than for me to trust what I'm actually seeing and reading in the Bible. The closer I examine the evidence at hand (Half Dome) and the Bible (the New Testament being the most authoritative historical record of antiquity the world has known), the more logical and reasonable and sound my trust that Jesus is God becomes.

What really closes the deal for me is that this image of Jesus on Half Dome has the mighty shout and intention of wrath. The image of the beast serves to bring the story together, but I'm riveted to the image of the mighty shout written of in the Holy Bible describing a specific action of God Almighty when He comes at the end of our world—shouting! What more do we need to know or see to identify God—His actual coming? What happens if I wait until then to figure this out?

The Holy Bible records Jesus as saying, "I have manifested Your name to the men whom You gave Me out of the world…" (John 17:6), and "...He who has seen Me has seen the Father..." (John 14:9). It was written about Jesus that, "For in [Christ] all the fullness of Deity dwells in bodily form" (Colossians 2:9). "By common confession, great is the mystery of godliness: [Jesus] was revealed in the flesh, Was vindicated in the spirit, Seen by angels, Proclaimed among the nations, Believed on in the world, Taken up in glory" (1 Timothy 3:16). Jesus said, "I and the Father are one" (John 10:30).

Three separate sources—the Ten Commandments, the Gospel accounts of Jesus, and the sign upon Half Dome; together form God's desire that we worship only God—as Jesus. The supernatural hand of God is pointing to Jesus. Jesus has been recorded as saying He is God. This is all tangible evidence verifying Jesus as being God. Jesus is God! This conclusion is a rational, logical, sane, sensible, sound, coherently linked fact. Not only is God revealed to us spiritually, but knowing God is also based on logic and physical observation. My only bias I am aware of is being passionate about reality. My search for the truth about God has led me to this point. I really don't know what else can honestly be concluded? It may not be fully conveyed through my writing, but I still struggle to come to terms with this reality. After all, I'm human, sinful, and selfish. Still, I must accept the truth about reality. It is the whole point of my search.

I will continue putting forth the effort to better understand what the Bible and Jesus are all about. In turn I know I will struggle less and less. This is my hunch. So far, everything revealed by God is more than good. It is a powerful revelation! And the repercussion of Jesus being God means the words of Jesus stand as being ultimate truth. In regards to the two greatest commandments Jesus spoke of, I paraphrase: Love God and love others; He also said, "On these two commandments depend the whole Law and the Prophets." Jesus confirmed the Septuagint and its prophets as being valid. God confirmed the Law and the Prophets through Jesus as being the truth about God. This links the Bible to God as being God's written word. Therefore, the Bible can be trusted as ultimate truth. My uncertainty about the validity of the Bible ends here. I trust the Bible as being true. It's now a matter of learning all that is contained within it.

The Distinction of Jesus

I have been a little confused when I read Jesus referring to Himself as the "Son of God." At first, my natural train of thought is to think of God birthing Jesus into existence, either as a messenger of God or as a human being, or both. The name "Son of God" doesn't seem to position Jesus as being God. The Gospel according to John in chapter 3:16 describes Jesus as God's "…only begotten Son…" In studying, this essentially means "the only one of its kind." Jesus was fully human, and fully divine according to Colossians 2:9, "For in Him all the fullness of Deity dwells in bodily form." If I stop at the "Son" of God I am led to think of a son or daughter being born of parents. I'd assume that God is God, and Jesus was born or created from God. But I find this isn't the case.

The distinction of Jesus is like no other being. I read that, "In the beginning was the Word, and the Word was with God, and the Word was God. He was in the beginning with God. All things came into being through Him, and apart from Him nothing came into being that has come into being. In Him was life, and the life was the Light of men. The Light shines in the darkness, and the darkness did not comprehend it" (John 1:1-5). Jesus is the "He" and the "Him" here. "And the word became flesh, and dwelt among us…" (John 1:14). The Bible testifies that Jesus is the "Word" who was at the beginning with God. I read again that Jesus said, "I and the Father are one" (John 10:30), and He also said, "...He who has seen Me has seen the Father..."

According to the Bible, Jesus was not born of God like you or me. It's written that, as a virgin, Mary became miraculously pregnant. At the time, she was engaged to a man named Joseph. They were to be married. The skeptical part of me says they most likely created the story of "immaculate conception" because back then they'd be in big trouble for having sex before they were married. But the Bible accounts it this way:

> "Now the birth of Jesus Christ was as follows: when His mother Mary had been betrothed [engaged to be married] to Joseph, before they came together [had sex] she was found to be with child [pregnant] by the Holy Spirit. And Joseph her husband, being a righteous man and not wanting to disgrace her, planned to send her away secretly. But when he had considered this, behold, an angel of the Lord appeared to him in a dream, saying, 'Joseph, son of David, do not be afraid to take Mary as your wife; for the Child who has been conceived in her is of the Holy Spirit. She will bear a Son; and you shall call His name Jesus, for He will save His people from their sins.' Now all this took place to fulfill what was spoken by the Lord through the prophet: 'BEHOLD, THE VIRGIN SHALL BE WITH CHILD AND SHALL BEAR A SON, AND THEY SHALL CALL HIS NAME IMMANUEL,' which translated means, 'GOD WITH US.' And Joseph awoke from his sleep and did as the angel of the Lord commanded him, and took *Mary* as his wife, but kept her a virgin until she gave birth to a Son; and he called His name Jesus" (Matthew 1:18-25).

What an amazing report! This was the way God chose to enter the earth realm, becoming a physical human being named Jesus. And to learn that Jesus always existed prior to His earthly birth is unimaginable. Even though it's clear and logical to understand that Jesus is God, *how* this is possible proves more difficult to take in, if it even can be comprehended. To me, the best way I can begin to grasp this is to relate to the concept of my automobile. I don't really understand exactly how the fuel I put in the gas tank and the key I turn equals me driving somewhere, but it does, and so I drive. I understand there is an engine inside that uses fuel for power, but I can't begin to explain the combustion process and how to produce the fuel it uses. Though I may not understand how it's physically possible for Jesus to be God, I see the facts saying He is God and so I accept. The entirety of God runs deeper than any abyss. How can I say the way Jesus got here is unreasonable? How can I say how Jesus is able to be God is impossible?

Jesus spoke, saying, "...I am the way, and the truth, and the life; no one comes to the Father but through Me" (John 14:6). In the same chapter He tells us, "I will ask the Father, and He will give you another Helper, that He may be with you forever; *that is* the Spirit of truth...I will not leave you as orphans; I will come to you...He who has My commandments and keeps them is the one who loves Me; and he who loves Me will be loved by My Father, and I will love him and will disclose Myself to him...If anyone loves Me, he will keep My word; and My Father will love him, and We will come to him and make Our abode with him" (John 14:16-18, 21, 23). In just a single chapter in John's gospel, Jesus refers to Himself, to the Father in heaven, and the Spirit, all as being the same, yet distinct. I don't know if I will ever fully comprehend how this is physically possible, but God is God and who I am to think God is incapable of anything? I realize I must simply accept certain things as being reality without holding the architectural design in my hands to view. I'm brought to this point of observation: it's not only possible Jesus is God—it is the case.

And what did Jesus come to do? His mission was clear: "For God so loved the world, that He gave His only begotten Son, that whoever believes in Him shall not perish, but have eternal life. For God did not send the Son into the world to judge the world, but that the world might be saved through Him. He who believes in Him is not judged; he who does not believe has been judged already, because he has not believed in the name of the only begotten Son of God. This is the judgment, that the Light has come into the world, and men loved the darkness rather than the Light, for their deeds were evil. For everyone who does evil hates the Light, and does not come to the light for fear that his deeds will be exposed. But he who practices the truth comes to the Light, so that his deeds may be manifested as having been wrought in God" (John 3:16-21).

In essence, God "gave" Himself so that we would have eternal life. Our failure to obey God puts us in the position of needing to be saved, "for all have sinned and fall short of the glory of God" (Romans 3:23). "...[T]hrough one man sin entered into the world, and death through sin, and so death spread to all men, because all sinned…death reigned from Adam until Moses, even over those who had not sinned in the likeness of the offense of Adam…For if by the transgression of the one, death reigned through the one, much more those who receive the abundance of grace and of the gift of righteousness will reign in life through the One, Jesus Christ. So then as through one transgression there resulted condemnation to all men, even so through one act of righteousness there resulted justification of life to all men. For as through one man's disobedience the many were made sinners, even so through the obedience of the One the many will be made righteous. The Law came in so that the transgression would increase; but where sin increased, grace abounded all the more, so that, as sin reigned in death, even so grace would reign through righteousness to eternal life through Jesus Christ our Lord" (Romans 5:12, 14, 17-21).

Sin entered through disobedience and brought death. The Law (the Ten Commandments) was given by God to reveal our need for redemption. Jesus came to redeem us from death. As I peel back the layers, He is shown to be waiting at the gate of the Father God in heaven. He said, "I am the door; if anyone enters through Me, he will be saved, and will go in and out and find pasture" (John 10:9). God, through Jesus, forgives and saves. The sacrificial death of Jesus makes it possible for anyone to inherit eternal life with God—anyone who will trust in Jesus as his or her Savior. And with this said, it is still somewhat puzzling that Jesus had to be crucified and had to die at all. God being God, I would imagine God has better options than to subject Himself to such brutality and tragedy.

Did He really have to die?

When I study my photographs of Half Dome, in between Jesus and the beast, a faint image draws me in. I'm not exactly sure what to make of it. I stare and stare, and see almost a figure hanging—arms up, body vertical below, and head drooping.

Of everything I've seen up to this point in this sign being displayed, for me it's fitting for this faint image to symbolize Jesus on the cross. After all, it is the one thing articulated by the Bible as standing between the furious wrath of God to come and evil (or sin). I'm not emphatically saying I see Jesus on the cross here,

but I've been gripped by what hangs in between the fury of God and the wickedness of evil on Half Dome. In a good sense we also are theoretically between God and the beast. I feel the center of this image upon this rock, there between God and Satan, may hold a mystery. I'm not exactly sure what to make of this image. I just know something is there speaking to me.

At face value, it seems paradoxical to me that God came to earth and lived as man to end up crucified by His creation. But the Book of Romans in the Bible thoroughly assembles the reason:

"For while we were still helpless, at the right time Christ died for the ungodly. For one will hardly die for a righteous man; though perhaps for the good man someone would dare even to die. But God demonstrates His own love toward us, in that while we were yet sinners, Christ died for us. Much more then, having now been justified by His blood, we shall be saved from the wrath *of God* through Him. For if while we were enemies we were reconciled to God through the death of His Son, much more, having been reconciled, we shall be saved by His life. And not only this, but we also exult in God through our Lord Jesus Christ, through whom we have now received the reconciliation" Therefore, just as through one man sin entered into the world, and death through sin, and so death spread to all men, because all sinned—for until the Law sin was in the world, but sin is not imputed when there is no law. Nevertheless death reigned from Adam until Moses, even over those who had not sinned in the likeness of the offense of Adam, who is a type of Him who was to come. But the free gift is not like the transgression. For if by the transgression of the one the many died, much more did the grace of God and the gift by the grace of the one Man, Jesus Christ, abound to the many. The gift is not like *that which came* through the one who sinned; for on the one hand the judgment *arose* from one *transgression* resulting in condemnation, but on the other hand the free gift *arose* from many transgressions resulting in justification. For if by the transgression of the one, death reigned through the one, much more those who receive the abundance of grace and of the gift of righteousness will reign in life through the One, Jesus Christ. So then as through one transgression there resulted condemnation to all men, even so through one act of righteousness there resulted justification of life to all men. For as through the one man's disobedience the many were made sinners, even so through the obedience of the One the many will be made righteous. The Law came in so that the transgression would increase; but where sin increased, grace abounded all the more, so that, as sin reigned in death, even so grace would reign through righteousness to eternal life through Jesus Christ our Lord" (Romans 5:6-21).

This Biblical passage teaches me what the death of Jesus was all about and why it was necessary. I see that the shed blood of Jesus was a method to justify my ungodly self before God to escape His wrath. The life of Jesus is God's way of reconciling my fallen relationship with God due to sin and disobedience—everyone's fallen relationship since birth, remaining unredeemed until trust in Christ restores our relationship with God. This is according to God. Death came through the first person to walk the earth, but eternal life is made possible once again through Jesus.

When I read for a second time, "For God so loved the world, that He gave His only begotten Son, that whoever believes in Him shall not perish, but have eternal life" (John 3:16), I better understand the how and why of this, that Jesus, not only came to earth, but came to die on earth for anyone who calls upon Him as Savior. I realize this includes me. Just because I don't fully process why life is this way; why God's creation is now tainted with sin; why life took this course; I very much appreciate being aware of it and the fact God cares enough to humble Himself down into our plight to rescue us.

It would be years and years later from when I had initially began studying my earliest photographs of these image upon Half Dome and reading the Bible about who Jesus is, that I really began to see and understand the overwhelming significance of His death upon the cross. With the capability of high-resolution photographs, details continue unfolding. As I read the Bible about Jesus and His death and examine these remarkable images, their story meshes deeper. I read what has been written. I observe what has been carved. And as I look much, much closer to the image in the center of the wall, I see what appears to be two feet, hanging, almost as if pinned, with what may even be fluid dripping from them?

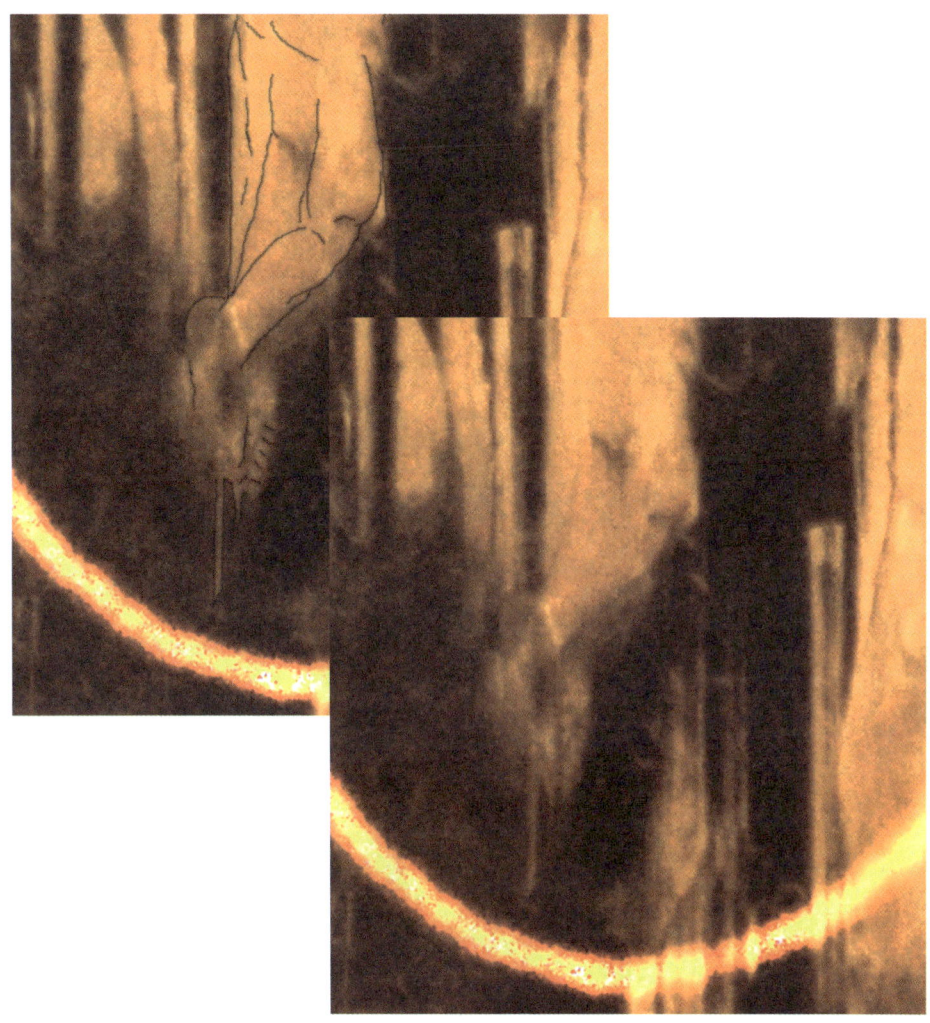

Then I follow the foot to the ankle, up to the knees, and to what looks like a shrouded body from head to knee.

His head appears to rest upon a folded cloth. Is it just me, or am I really seeing a body positioned vertically, covered with cloth and feet fastened together? To me the legs and feet portray a classic portrayal of Jesus on the cross.

The upper body here might depict how one could have been prepared for burial at the time of Jesus with a shroud. At this point, if this is really what I'm seeing, it's not farfetched for this to be Jesus.

"And when they had crucified Him, they divided up His garments among themselves by casting lots…And Jesus cried out again with a loud voice, and yielded up His spirit. And behold, the veil of the temple was torn in two from top to bottom; and

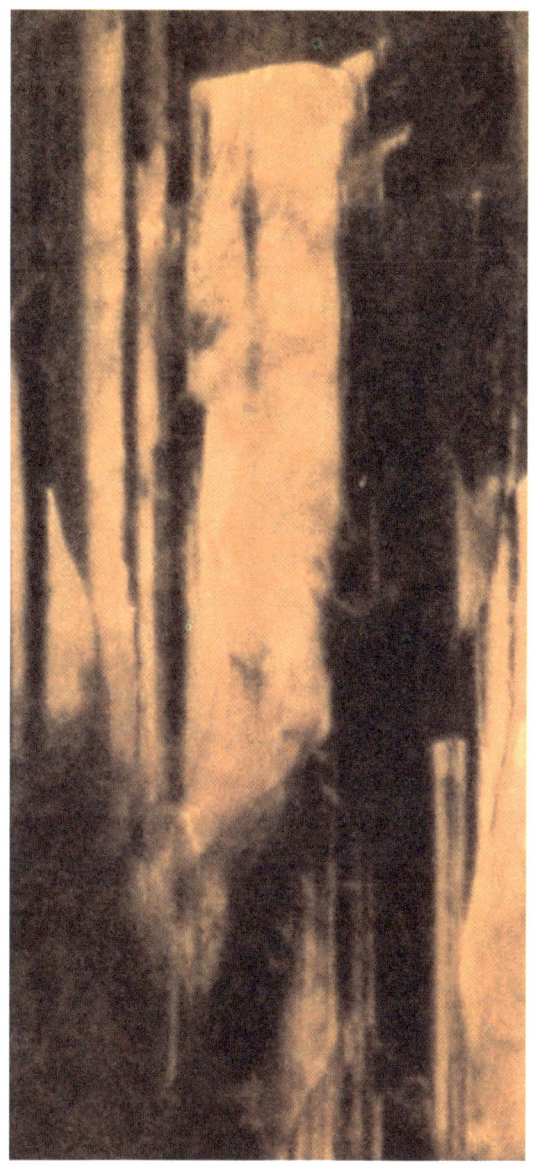

the earth shook and the rocks were split....When it was evening, there came a rich man from Arimathea, named Joseph, who himself had also become a disciple of Jesus. This man went to Pilate and asked for the body of Jesus...And Joseph took the body and wrapped it in a clean linen cloth, and laid it in his own new tomb, which he had hewn out in the rock..." (Matthew 27:35, 50-51, 57-60).

This is the account of Jesus being wrapped in cloth. If Half Dome truly holds the image of Jesus hanging and covered, we do know that at some point in His life He did in fact hang on the cross and was wrapped in a cloth. It does not surprise me that God would include this image upon Half Dome because it is the most significant event in history apart from His resurrection.

Jesus' death upon the cross is not parochial. He "died for all, so that they who live might no longer live for themselves, but for Him who died and rose again on their behalf…Therefore if anyone is in Christ, he is a new creature; the old things passed away; behold, new things have come" (Romans 5:15, 17). Jesus "…knew no sin *to be* sin on our behalf, so that we might become the righteousness of God in Him" (2 Corinthians 5:21). Jesus "…rescued us from the domain of darkness…" (Colossians 1:13), and, "…if you confess with your mouth Jesus as Lord, and believe in your heart that God raised Him from the dead, you will be saved" (Romans 10:9). "…DEATH IS SWALLOWED UP in victory. O death, where is your victory? O death, where is your sting?" (1 Corinthians 15:54-55). Jesus came to "…reconcile…" us "…to God through the cross, by it having put to death the enmity" between He and Satan (Ephesians 2:16).

In a great sense God has already judged the sin of the world through Christ's death on the cross, offering forgiveness and eternal life. But it's clear I must still make the choice to trust in Jesus for giving Himself in place of my sin. Death loses its "sting" because of salvation from Christ. The Bible records Satan's loss of power and authority, all because of what Jesus has done. This knowledge compels me to not only draw distinctions with myself, but now with the culture at large. My mind is churning to reason with past and present observations. I can't help but to recognize the objective reality around me. I can't avoid assessing the character of my culture and everything streaming through the media. I can't escape discerning my actions and the actions of others for what they are—positive, negative, good, or evil. I can't escape the realization of my own sin—because Jesus has said I am in need of forgiveness. It's like I woke up from some matrix of misconception to suddenly see the raw nature of reality. It's impossible at this point not to process how this knowledge of God and Jesus and Satan affects everything. It is becoming ever apparent that everything is connected in some way. Life's complex equation of truth is emerging as elementary.

I realize Satan can only rely on deception to trick me into believing his authority still stands. The only control he is allowed is the control we betray our own selves into giving away. But realizing and living according to what God has done for us through the cross renders Satan powerless. According to the Holy Bible eminent damnation clings to my soul because I have lacked the willingness to trust that Jesus can bring me back from Satan's grip, dying as a sacrifice and being resurrected.

The battle between Jesus and Satan still rages, but now it's centered on winning the souls of humankind. It's clear to me now more than ever that you and I are the center of attention. Satan knows God has set the Day of Judgment, in which all sin and rebellion will be destroyed. Satan knows the time is short, as the Bible explains and foretells: "From…[the]…mouth…[of Jesus]…comes a sharp sword …" (Revelation 19:15). "And the devil…was thrown into the lake of fire and brimstone…and…will be tormented day and night forever and ever" (Revelation 20:10).

The victory is set as God's and the defeat of Satan approaches. The only way to remain alive apart from hell is through salvation in Christ. Jesus claims victory. Satan nonetheless still fights. If there really "is no neutral ground in the universe" like C. S. Lewis has written, and "every square inch," and "every split second, is claimed by God and counter-claimed by Satan," I must have some role in this battle while God and the devil go head to head. It is evident that this battle surrounds me. By choosing the side of God my first step has to be surrendering my life to Christ. What an ironic twist of fate to think that surrendering leads to victory. I would never have guessed this to be the case when I set out on my journey for these answers I now can't seem to stop from coming.

Recovering Life

Accepting all of this is not easy or natural. I innately resist. Maybe it's sin, or maybe it's just me—both perhaps. Nonetheless, even with everything I know so far I struggle to fully bring myself to agree that God is somehow contained within a physical person named Jesus. I've inquired with others about what they know. I wrestle through the Bible, trying to make more sense of this implication. But the more I read about Jesus, the more I see how the almighty God, who's out there somewhere, relates with us through Jesus. The story goes: by God becoming Man, God took on our earthly shell and walked the same dirt, faced our challenges, and directly shares something in common with us and things I go through. Maybe God being God did not need to go this far by dying, but I now see that I am forever indebted because of the fact God did.

Even with the truth looking me square in the eyes it's still not easy for me to surrender to Jesus. I mostly wrestle with this idea because I don't want to give in until I'm completely overwhelmed with realistic, fact-based truth. But my back is up against the wall because God sculpted Jesus onto a giant granite rock reaching into the sky, directing me to Jesus. I am being stripped of any excuses I've had. The Bible confirms the descriptions of Jesus upon Half Dome. The words "Half Dome" might not be written in black and white, but the Bible tells of stones crying out; it speaks of a Man being transfigured, wearing a crown of thorns and of golden light, and His face being as the appearance of lightening and eye like a flame of fire. And, of course, having a shout—the mighty shout! God even put His archrival in the picture.

Half Dome professes the Bible. The Bible confirms the images upon Half Dome. And since they identify each other, my doubts about both sources originating from God are being wiped away—the Spirit of God has inspired both. I know the supernatural sign on Half Dome can only be from God, and because it pays tribute to the Bible, the Bible is demonstrated as being a trustworthy account of reality— objective truth. I think in essence the truth has wrestled *me* to the ground. The truth has pinned *me* down! Even in this position I battle giving my heart to Jesus.

I recognize how I've chosen against God's will at times and that these tendencies will potentially ruin me. If God calls destructive behavior sin, then sin it is. Who am I to argue with God about this? If God gives me a plan to live, but my choices ultimately cultivate death, I have to accept God's view of my decision as disobedience to His desires. After all, God has my best interest in mind—life. And I ultimately desire to live, forever. But if "nature took its course" I would die in sin, being eternally separated from God. "For the wages of sin is death…" (Romans 6:23). My current state, including the state of humankind, is a medical emergency. With each day that passes my final day approaches—you, yours. And here on earth, each day lived without knowing God is one more day my life remains in jeopardy and unfulfilled.

The hand of God through Jesus Christ reaches out, offering the life-saving cure for eternal suffering. A lifeline is in place to take hold of and, "…if [I] confess with [my] mouth Jesus *as* Lord, and believe in [my] heart that God raised Him from the dead, [I] will be saved" (Romans 10:9). "…[W]hoever believes in [Jesus] shall not perish, but have eternal life" (John 3:16). Even though the payment for sin is death, "…the free gift of God is eternal life in Christ Jesus our Lord" (Romans 6:23).

I feel a deep connection with God—love from God even though I've done wrong. I'm so glad God can be known. So I can't help but to profess and confess, "Jesus, be Lord of my life! I trust you came to die as a sacrifice for my sin, and rose from the dead. I don't fully comprehend how you are God, but I trust I can honor and adore you. I see my redemption as a free gift from You, that I can receive only through You. Even though many people pray and hope for my soul, ultimately it amounts to me approaching You, asking You for the gift of salvation. Jesus, I realize You desire a relationship with me, even with my sister, brother, mother and father, and everyone I know and care about. But I'm asking right now for a relationship with You. I trust Your death upon the cross was the sacrifice for the sin of all people—and me. I choose to understand Your rising from the grave reveals the conquering of death, and offers eternal life as I trust in You. Thank you for Your mercy."

I don't believe magic is involved here or a secret formula connecting me with God. All I can ever do is talk to God with a sincere heart and know God because I ask this from Him. Even if this makes me a Christian now, I'm okay with this. It's all about the Lord God anyway. I make a vow to know the Lord Jesus and seek His mercy to follow me all of my days. I realize there is nothing apart from this I can do to be saved from eternal damnation. No good works can save me—nothing. It's only by the confession of my heart to Jesus that rescues me from the future sufferings of hell. "For by grace you have been saved through faith; and that not of yourselves, *it is* the gift of God; not as a result of works, so that no one may boast" (Ephesians 2:8-9). I just receive this gift offered and rebuke any guilty feelings that stand between God and me. It doesn't matter what anyone has done in life. Whatever we've done is not enough to keep the love of God from saving. Heaven awaits our response to the Savior.

The extraordinary aspect to salvation is that I cannot repay God for it. I can only live a life devoted to the Lord and contend for obedience to God as Jesus has led. All there is to offer is myself to others in Jesus' name and present to God a living faith. "For just as the body without *the* spirit is dead, so also faith without works is dead" (James 2:26). By sincerely confessing trust in Jesus, my heart will be dedicated to God and Christ followed. This is the truth. I understand mistakes will be made, but I can "Consider it all joy…when you encounter various trials, knowing that the testing of your faith produces endurance" (James 1:2-3). "For a righteous man falls seven times, and rises again…" (Proverbs 24:16). Jesus said, "So do not worry about tomorrow; for tomorrow will care for itself. Each day has enough trouble of its own" (Matthew 6:34). "…LOVE THE LORD YOUR GOD WITH ALL YOUR HEART, AND WITH ALL YOUR SOUL, AND WITH ALL YOUR MIND, AND WITH ALL YOUR STRENGTH" (Mark 12:30). This is the assurance of eternal life, in Jesus' name.

Warm Waters

I took part in the criticism of Christians over the years and heard a lot of it from others as well, "They don't measure up. Hypocrites. They're weird, and delusional. They aren't rational, and base their faith on only feelings and hope. Christians are intolerant to believe Jesus is the only way to God, or heaven." I surely did not set out to become a Christian. I just set out to know the truth but found Jesus at its core. What is a person to do except honor the truth by living according to it? What I am supposed to do other than accept and receive it, and appreciate life for everything it is. I am alive after all, and now eternally secure. What else am I supposed to do except what I am now doing?

In light of the criticisms and expectations, I think the Christian way of life will be the most challenging. One, because aspiring to live a Godly life is sure to have its tests and trials. I'm sure I will fail and feel like giving up. Two, it will be challenging because of the belittling and contempt from people who aren't

Christians. Maybe being born and living in San Francisco has greatly colored my view of Christians and how Christians are perceived. I know it's not like this everywhere in the world. But it's like this here, where I live and also in so many other places too, even to much greater extremes.

To all the critics of Christianity, I say, come show us how to be a better Christian. Come demonstrate before the presence of God more of who Jesus is and live it out. Don't try to deceive me, don't control me, just honestly teach me the truth about God as a follower of Christ, as someone who will trust in Jesus. Come help set others free who are in the bondage of deception. Come and reveal more of who Jesus is, and let truth be your guide—"…prove yourselves doers of the word, and not merely hearers who delude themselves" (James 1:22). Don't sit on the sidelines heckling about what Christians do wrong. Come and demonstrate what's right according to what's true.

All are welcome to come and live this out. The Bible says that, "…God our Savior…desires all men to be saved and come to the knowledge of the truth" (1 Timothy 2:3-4). You are free to demonstrate how to connect with God by the witness and power of your own relationship with Christ. Each individual on this planet has the opportunity to walk the walk in a healthy, truthful, merciful, loving and just way. Anyone is free to promote positive ways and create a constructive and liberating environment for everyone.

Perhaps the last instance or series of injustices, committed in the name of God or Jesus by flawed human beings has got you turned off to Christ. It bothers me too. So let's move forward to live out the greatest charge: "…'GOD IS ONE LORD; AND YOU SHALL LOVE THE LORD YOUR GOD WITH ALL YOUR HEART, AND WITH ALL YOUR SOUL, AND WITH ALL YOUR MIND, AND WITH ALL YOUR STRENGTH.' The second is this, 'YOU SHALL LOVE YOUR NEIGHBOR AS YOURSELF.' There is no other commandment greater than these" (Mark 12:29-31). I found it much easier to shout my disapproval from the sidelines. But to join the game, that's where life's at. So instead of running down the list of what I saw wrong, I've come in to try and demonstrate what is right.

What could be holding you back? I have to ask because the message on Half Dome couldn't just be for me. Just like my dream, I feel that others are meant to see this too—even hear from God. What is it saying to you? The Bible is not my own private book. You too must have your own stirrings in your own heart.

All of this truth being revealed by God isn't exclusive to me. So then why do we hold back from committing our life to God? Is it fear, or shame, guilt, pride, or willful sin—feelings of unworthiness? So what, if we are ashamed of things we've done in secret or even in public; so what if we may go to church only once in a while or not at all, living in a state of defeat for whatever reason or influence; so what if our brain says we don't deserve the love and forgiveness of God—and we don't; but so what to it all! So what! Because God is greater than all of it—our problems and sin!

It doesn't matter that we are weak, guilty, prideful, or feeling helpless. God remains by our side. In spite of these things I choose to draw life from the Lord who's been waiting for my own mighty shout to Him. Jesus lives to give His Spirit, to rescue. We can place hope and trust in Him. Discouragement, how ever real, ultimately doesn't have a chance of surviving in Christ, because God has not forsaken us. I am assured of this when I read, "…He who began a good work in you will perfect it until the day of Christ Jesus" (Philippians 1:6). I really don't think it's about my life being perfect, but rather God working in and through my life to continuously make it better. I can pray for help that, "…the God of peace…equip [me] in every good thing to do His will, working in us that which is pleasing in His sight, through Jesus Christ…" (Hebrews 13:20-21). It matters the most that I continuously look to God as the source of direction and hope. God invites people to, "…receive a kingdom which cannot be shaken…" (Hebrews 12:28). So what do you say? Come in, the water is warm.

Rules of Engagement

Back in 33 A.D., the week before Jesus was crucified there is an account of Jesus entering into the city of Jerusalem for what would be His last time before being put to death on the cross. Jesus, along with thousands of people approached the city to celebrate the long-held Jewish tradition of Passover—their freedom and life in God. A large part of this crowd was hailing and praising Jesus as He walked toward Jerusalem. "As He was going, they were spreading their coats on the road. As soon as he was approaching, near the descent of the Mount of Olives, the whole crowd of the disciples began to praise God joyfully with a loud voice for all the miracles which they had seen, shouting: 'Blessed is the King who comes in the name of the Lord; Peace in heaven and glory in the highest!' Some of the Pharisees in the crowd said to Him, 'Teacher, rebuke Your disciples.' But Jesus answered, "I tell you, if these become silent, the stones will cry out!" (Luke 19:36-40). Jesus even spoke of "things which make for peace", as being "hidden from" their "eyes" (Luke 19:42).

What I gather taking place in the Scripture here is that even though people may stop praising the Lord the earth would still speak of God's glory. God is even able to make plain things hidden. I see Half Dome as a granite monolith shouting "Jesus!" yet being hidden from our eyes throughout the years. This remarkable manifestation of stone cries out the glory of God, calling us through Half Dome to the Lord. It is written, "Therefore let us draw near with confidence to the throne of grace, so that we may receive mercy and find grace to help in time of need" (Hebrews 4:16). I'm in total admiration of God that He has helped me to see and given much for me to come to know Him. This truly awakens me. I sense now it's my turn to give of myself whatever I can to God. The most accurate way to determine what I can be doing for God in regards to the battle is to study not only the life and words of Jesus, but also the words of His original messengers who established the New Testament.

About forty-three percent of the New Testament writings consist of the four Gospels, which focus on the account of Jesus' life. This means about fifty-seven percent of the New Testament is composed mainly of letters by apostles who wrote about Jesus, His divinity, and how to live in light of Him. Of this fifty-seven percent, about thirty-four percent are the writings of the Apostle Paul. He not only had much to say about the battle between God and the devil, he lived it. The Apostle Paul, in my opinion should be able to best define what the role of a Christian looks like. I learned that Paul, whose name was formerly Saul, was on a mission to kill those proclaiming Jesus as God. Saul was a religious leader who believed the followers of Jesus were spreading lies about who Saul understood God to be. Then one day on his way to continue his persecution of Christians, Saul learned of who Jesus is.

As [Saul] was traveling…approaching Damascus, and suddenly a light from heaven flashed around him; and he fell to the ground and heard a voice saying to him, 'Saul, Saul, why are you persecuting *Me*?' And he said, 'Who are You, Lord?' And He *said*, 'I am Jesus whom you are persecuting" (Acts 9:3-5).

From this moment forward, one of the fiercest opponents of Christ became one of His greatest advocates all the way to his own persecution as a Christian. The Apostle Paul fully engaged the battle he found himself in the middle of—between God and the devil. Surely Paul has something to say about how to live in the midst of this battle between good and evil.

Paul wrote, "…we are ambassadors for Christ, as though God were making an appeal through us…" (2 Corinthians 5:20). A Christian is to represent heaven on earth. So not only should I see myself as a citizen of the nation in which I live, I am a citizen of God's kingdom. The apostle Paul encourages, "…by the mercies of God, to present your bodies a living and holy sacrifice, acceptable to God, *which is your spiritual service of worship*" (Romans 12:1). My first opportunity of service to God is to present myself as a "living and holy sacrifice acceptable to God." This amounts to a life being set apart for want God desires.

Paul goes on to say, "And do not be conformed to this world, but be transformed by the renewing of your mind, so that you may prove what the will of God is, that which is good and acceptable and perfect. For through the grace given to me I say to everyone among you not to think more highly of himself than he ought to think; but to think so as to have sound judgment, as God has allotted to each a measure of faith" (Romans 12:1-3). Paul challenges me to be transformed and prove the will of God and to remain humble in the process, having sound judgment.

Apostle Paul speaks specifically to the battle between God and the devil. He says, "…be strong in the Lord and in the strength of His might. Put on the full armor of God, so that you will be able to stand firm against the schemes of the devil. For our struggle is not against flesh and blood, but against the rulers, against the powers, against the world forces of this darkness, against the spiritual *forces* of wickedness in the heavenly *places*. Therefore, take up the full armor of God, so that you will be able to resist in the evil day, and having done everything, to stand firm. Stand firm therefore, HAVING GIRDED YOUR LOINS WITH TRUTH, and HAVING PUT ON THE BREASTPLATE OF RIGHTEOUSNESS, and having SHOD YOUR FEET WITH THE PREPARATION OF THE GOSPEL OF PEACE; in addition to all, taking up the shield of faith with which you will be able to extinguish all the flaming arrows of the evil *one*. And TAKE THE HELMET OF SALVATION, and the sword of the Spirit, which is the word of God. With all prayer and petition pray at all times in the Spirit, and with this in view, be on the alert with all perseverance and petition for all the saints…make known with boldness the mystery of the gospel" (Ephesians 6:10-19).

Paul lays out a descriptive strategy for me to use. He calls me to put on the full armor of God. Wow! It's astounding to look back at Half Dome and visually see a snapshot of this colossal tension between spiritual forces. The spirit realm breaks into the terra firma of Yosemite allowing for a glimpse of true reality. There is no denying we are in the middle of a great struggle and should be prepared to deal with it. And as I carefully examine this passage of Scripture I search the deeper meanings of his words. I'm drawn to hunt down each aspect of the armor to better understand what it means. I draw the distinction that my feet can be shod with the principle of 1 Peter 3:15, to "…sanctify Christ as Lord in your hearts, always *being* ready to make a defense to everyone who asks you to give an account for the hope that is in you, yet with gentleness and reverence." I have received Christ in my heart, and now work to articulate the reasons for the eternal reality of God in my life.

My loins can be girded with John 14:6: "Jesus said…I am the way, and the truth, and the life; no one comes to the Father but through Me." This is the powerful truth I have taken on by receiving Jesus as God. This reality fortifies me. I searched out Isaiah 51:7 as being a breastplate of righteousness. It says, "…Do not fear the reproach of man, Nor be dismayed at their revilings." This reminds me to put God's will first and that I am able to endure the criticisms of other people. When I read "In the beginning was the Word, and the Word was with God, and the Word was God…And the Word became flesh, and dwelt among us…" (John 1:1, 14), I realize the Bible is the Word (the sword of the Spirit) I am to apply in my life.

I put on the helmet of salvation by knowing, "For God so loved the world, that he gave His only begotten Son, that whoever believes in Him shall not perish, but have eternal life" (John 3:16). I must never forget I am God's now. The reality of salvation will protect my mind from any doubt that God would let my spirit die. I sought out the shield of faith and discovered the verses of Romans 8:1-2: "Therefore, there is now no condemnation for those who are in Christ Jesus. For the law of the Spirit of life in Christ Jesus has set you free from the law of sin and death." God does not want me carrying the guilt of my sin that would weigh me down. Jesus carried it to the cross for me and has set me free to live for God.

I see these scriptures as principles and encouragement for me to rely on within this spiritual battle. I'm so new to this way of life and choosing to put on the full armor of God will help me establish a sure footing in reality. Paul's analogy for preparation in the spiritual war is invaluable. This perspective heightens my awareness of reality all the more. Jesus said, "You are the light of the world. A city set on a hill cannot be hidden; nor does *anyone* light a lamp and put it under a basket, but on the lampstand, and it gives light to all who are in the house. Let your light shine before men in such a way that they may see your good works, and glorify your Father who is in heaven" (Matthew 5:14-16). Jesus makes it clear that the reality of God should not be hidden. The words of Scripture are preparing me to be a healthy example to God's credit. This is a tall order at the very least. Trepidation knocks at my door when I think of being a light to others to help them know who God is. But if this is what God is calling me to do then I must have faith God will help me to do it.

Jesus said, "Ask, and it will be given to you; seek, and you will find; knock, and it will be opened to you. For everyone who asks receives, and he who seeks finds, and to him who knocks it will be opened" (Matthew 7:7-8). I know I'll be taking God up on this promise.

I am motivated by the author's letter to the Hebrew people to stay focused and make great strides with my life: "Therefore, since we have so great a cloud of witnesses surrounding us, let us also lay aside every encumbrance and the sin which so easily entangles us, and let us run with endurance the race that is set before us, fixing our eyes on Jesus, the author and perfecter of faith, who for the joy set before Him endured the cross, despising the shame, and has sat down at the right hand of the throne of God" (Hebrews 12:1-2). There is no turning back now.

Essential Observations

My direction in which to proceed is clear, but what am I really ready to do? What is my day-to-day walk supposed to look like? I mean do I walk around with "culture warrior" stamped on my forehead looking for spiritual skirmishes to engage in? I have a job. I have friends and family. I go to the store to buy food and clothes. I go to places like Yosemite and the beach. And along the way I hope to build my life into something better than it was yesterday. But what does it look like to stand against evil and make the right choices—the best choices? I still feel the need to close the gap of reason between the spirit and earth realm, and apply God's principles in the most practical ways. I know part of this means examining myself more closely and discerning the effect my choices have on my life. I'm drawn to drench my mind and spirit in the principles of God, but I want the result to be useful. I dread becoming some type of spiritual cuckoo bird having a hollow sound, ineffective when it comes to helping people and fostering positive and needed changes, in my life and the greater one surrounding me. I want my trust in Christ to yield the things people need to be all God intends us to be.

At the beginning of this book I posed the question as to whether or not religious faith is a cultural virus actually standing in the way of true enlightenment, or whether distrust in God is most dangerous. I think it depends on what we want as a world. If what we want is to avoid accepting the true reality out of a desire to live according to sheer imagination, for whatever reason, then trust in God would indeed be a virus. I think most of us would not opt for this. But on the other hand if we want to base life entirely upon a true reality then distrust in God would contradict our declaration to be real people. I don't think our faith in God will destroy us, but quite the opposite. Our relationship with God is what will help us.

I think faith in anything not grounded in reality potentially skews our ability to possess an accurate perception of reality. This type of foundational thinking could in turn advance a kind of "cultural illness" that would obstruct true progress and unity. It seems the wise thing to do is to base our life upon true reality, even in spite of things we don't like about our past. The opportunity to make right for old wrongs provides more hope than moving forward in obscurity. The past is past, but the future encourages resolution—even the promises of God. We've got to get past the animosity about the kingdom of God. Christ is proving to be on the throne of reality. This is God's doing. I think the way of true enlightenment is to align with this true reality. I think by doing this we can achieve the things God intends for us.

The Bible instructs me to have a clear head because my actions reap consequences: "For if anyone thinks he is something when he is nothing, he deceives himself. But each one must examine his own work…Do not be deceived, God is not mocked; for whatever a man sows, this he will also reap" (Galatians 6:3-4, 7). Newton's third law is the law of reciprocal actions. It states, "For every action force there is an equal, but opposite, reaction force." I'm not sure about the math of human relations and situations, but the choices made about them always seem to reap a result. The by-product of my life then produces positive or negative effects as a result of my choices. The factor of God's intervention definitely influences the equation, but my attitude, response, and intentions set my course. I hope the sum total of my life will be something good and helpful to others.

Whether it's acknowledged or not, a well-lived life is a result of being guided by the hand of God through His principles. The Holy Bible has got to be the most comprehensive resource identifying the principles of God, which logically represents the highest standard. I think the Bible can even be a resource to the high criterion of science. We're talking high, tangible standards on which to base the way humankind is designed to live. Jesus said, "…'It is written, 'MAN SHALL NOT LIVE ON BREAD ALONE, BUT ON EVERY WORD THAT PROCEEDS OUT OF THE MOUTH OF GOD'" (Matthew 4:4). This makes the Word of God the handbook of life.

I see no cosmic conflict between God and science. In fact, God stands up to the progress of science. Logic follows: if science is the study of reality, and God is reality, then at the center of science is God. Science simply has not yet achieved the tools to physically observe the spiritual realm—or may not be observing it correctly. Science and the spiritual don't clash, nor are they at odds with each other. Individuals clash, and lead others to clash. All minds have the opportunity of remaining open to the most wonderful range of future possibilities we have yet to dream about, even when it leads us to one particular conclusion, and even to Christ. No person should allow skepticism to stop his or her mind from observing reality because we want reality to be something in particular. It may turn out that way, but our job is to understand it and affect positive change wherever possible.

Through all my study of the Bible and reasoning about life, the theme that keeps coming to mind is: examine and discern as much of reality as possible. The Bible consistently promotes the absolute awareness of reality. This means having to call things what they are. If I am asked by someone to discern or distinguish the essential foundation of my relationship with God I would report my findings, "…that Christ died for our sins according to the Scriptures, and that He was buried, and that He was raised on the third day according to the Scriptures, and that He appeared…" to the Apostles and many, many other people (1 Corinthians 15:3-5), and "that if you confess with your mouth Jesus *as* Lord, and believe in your heart that God raised Him from the dead, you will be saved" (Romans 10:9). Essential to this act of will is, knowing, "For by grace you have been saved through faith; and not of yourselves, *it is* the gift of God; not as a result of works…" (Ephesians 2:8-9). Understanding that Jesus is God in flesh according to John 1:1 and 1:14, is essential. This makes me a Christian.

And upon deeper examination I found these essential foundations demonstrate the absolute, essential nature that Biblical authors were inspired by God, leading to the inerrancy of the Bible, the virgin birth of Jesus as Biblically attested to, and the second coming of Jesus for which we wait. Through all of these essential foundations, one can observe the Father, the Son, and the Holy Spirit to identify the triune nature of the Godhead as being the central character of God. These primary essentials accurately represent as much as God has revealed about Himself. This access of essential truth being provided by God sends me forth with complete confidence about who God is to fulfill His plan for my life.

Sometimes I feel overwhelmed studying precept upon precept. It almost feels like I'm back in school learning lesson after lesson. But perhaps a test is coming and if I fail to observe the essential foundations that make up who I am, I fail to discern myself. And if I can't distinguish the aspects making up my own life, how would I ever be ready to engage the culture as the Apostle Paul has lain out? So I'm called to "Be diligent to present [my] self approved to God as a workman who does not need to be ashamed, accurately handling the word of truth" (2 Timothy 2:15). It has to be ingrained within me that God gives me the right to test everything in light of Biblical scriptures and reality, them against me. But this means I am obligated to be educated about Biblical truth. This equals effort on my part to do so. So perhaps I should see my learning as service back to God for His gift of grace upon my life. But it's so much more than this. This is God's way of equipping anyone who seeks after Him so they're not left helpless in the midst of His battle with the devil. In turn I gain skill.

God knows that the strategy of evil is to take advantage of gullible and naïve thinking—ignorance. The Lord does not want us to be powerless here. We are instructed to "Let no one deceive you with empty words…" (Ephesians 5:6). The Apostle Paul commended the people of Berea because "…these were more noble-minded…for they received the word with great eagerness, examining the Scriptures daily *to see* whether these things were so" (Acts 17:11). It is perfectly acceptable to verify the truth, even respectable. The initial steps of a Christian are to learn of God's ways. I find it not only to be exhilarating at times, but work as well.

But the Bible is shedding much light for wading through the waters of truth and deception. I'm learning to swim through the cultural confusion and callousness. The sign upon Half Dome is helping me to see the physical reality of God, and how to accurately reason the truth. I seek to inspect my own ways first, and then all else. The goal is to "…discern good and evil" (Hebrews 5:13-14).

The presence of evil has been fooling me into thinking that discerning a person's character and actions is to judge their soul. On this note, judging a person's soul is not our place, but only God's. For all other matters, I have the responsibility to distinguish the difference between safety and danger, that which is constructive and destructive, respect and disrespect, truth and deception. Jesus said, "Do not judge according to appearance, but judge with righteous judgment" (John 7:24). Paul said, "Test yourselves to *see* if you are in the faith; examine yourselves!" (2 Corinthians 13:5). Self-scrutiny is the key to a healthy life and, "…if we judged ourselves rightly, we would not be judged" (1 Corinthians 11:31).

It's not right for me to disregard my own issues, and attack someone else's. I need to "…first take the log out of [my] own eye, and then [I] will see clearly to take the speck out of…" (Matthew 7:5) someone else's eye. How can I see and discern situations and relationships when my perspective is impaired, greatly or otherwise. By developing a healthy self-government, much of life is more easily ordered. But poor self-government ultimately makes me the master architect of my struggles. Resolving personal problems stabilizes and strengthens my life. This is where blessing resides. Being a student of truth will help me get there.

The Bible is saying to be thoughtful, to "…walk as children of Light… trying to learn what is pleasing to the Lord…" (Ephesians 5:8, 10). Who among us is exempt from learning and practicing this? I can boldly grasp for answers I need because it is written, "…the Lord will give…understanding in everything" (2 Timothy 2:7). The truth is unwavering, and will remain. It cannot be destroyed. "For we can do nothing against the truth, but *only* for the truth" (2 Corinthians 13:8). Therefore, I can depend on truth to accept reality, in turn gaining wisdom. And as a student of reality my actions should lead over words, "…let us not love with word or tongue, but in deed and truth" (1 John 3:18). Jesus reminds, "…'See to it that you are not misled…'" (Luke 21:8). One of my main duties is to be prepared and equipped with truth. This is living with purpose. I must contend for my destiny, and tackle the obstacles that seek to distract and deceive me from it. The early Christian Paul put this way: "We *are* destroying speculations and every lofty thing raised up against the knowledge of God…" (2 Corinthians 10:5). This is the paramount reason to put on the full armor of God and become equipped with the principles of God—to know the truth and be set free and help set others free.

The Great Disconnect

The battle between light and darkness is heavy. Since I am now one who trusts in Christ and chooses to live by the Godly principles set in the Bible, I find yet another battle. It's not enough to struggle with myself, but now with my worldview in the public domain. Maybe my disorientation comes from not being sure how to represent the truth.

Am I supposed to now leave my worldview at the doorstep of my heart and home, and live my public life trying not to let my relationship with God influence my decisions? I know this is impossible, but I hear the "secular worldview" challenging Christians to do this. If I understand them correctly, it is acceptable to *call* myself a Christian as long as I don't let it be known publicly or make decisions based on my relationship with Christ. Honestly, I don't see how this is possible.

Who started the myth that says there must be separation between what one believes
and how one governs, or leads? I recognize the cultural battle aimed at removing
the acknowledgement of God from public life. By "public" I mean life out in the
open where everyone can see. It seems some people are greatly offended by the
proclamation and acknowledgement of God, especially anything associated with
Jesus. So it means this battle is aimed at me because the truth has inevitably led
me to take on a worldview under siege. But come on, everyone has some type of
worldview guiding his or her decisions—not just Christians. Show me an individual
with a mind and I'll show you their worldview. It's been said that justice is blind,
but even justice advocates justice. If justice were a person, his or her worldview
would be the very principles of what justice is made of. I'm trying to show that
there is a worldview behind every single person.

How can I *advocate* anything other than who I am, and God who I trust
in? I wouldn't be true to that which guides me. I wouldn't be true to myself. How
can anyone *be expected* to leave his or her spirit at the threshold of life and walk
anywhere or say anything without it? The notion itself is completely unrealistic. The
fact of the matter: everyone brings their worldview to the table of reason and when
ruling, and everyone acts upon it. Whether someone proclaims to be a Christian or
chooses to believe there is no God, both influence people and both make decisions
based on trusting their own worldview. Let's just be out with this.

Maybe you don't subscribe to any religious affiliation or even a specific
type of scientific reasoning or philosophy. But if you and I were to sit down with a
piece of paper to interview each other about what we think, and why we think, or
what we trust, we would end up with a clear picture of our individual worldview.
A crystal-clarity does exist as to what we trust in and why we make the choices
we do. It just has to be examined to uncover it. We can pinpoint what we think or
believe if we truly want to. Even if it's entirely original but never articulated until
now, it's still a worldview. It's the worldview you own. We could call it the religion
of "you" if you prefer. You may not attend church, or go to synagogue, or have any
official affiliation, but the religion of "you" is the daily guide you trust in.

I may not agree with your worldview and you may not agree with mine,
but that doesn't stop you from being influenced by yours, and me mine. And

regardless of what I hold to be true I must respect you as a person, and not insult or abuse you for what you believe. We could, however, reason together about the foundations of both our worldviews, helping each other to understand them. All in all, we both have worldviews—different, opposing, or the same. It's nothing personal. It's just the case.

But for whatever reason now that I'm a "Christian" it seems I'm supposed to keep my worldview to myself and not let it influence my decisions out in "public." Again, how is this possible? If I understand this right, "A judge who is a Christian on the Supreme Court better not let his or her relationship with Christ influence his or her decisions!" How would anyone be able to do this? Someone refer to any other judge who is not a Christian and explain to me how their worldview isn't influencing their decisions. It is! It's absurd to conclude otherwise. It's got to be Satan's strategy making me think twice about being Christian, pressuring me into choosing a path of less resistance? This is a genuine situation within our culture. This situation is also a major intersection where the spiritual rubber meets the earthly road. This issue makes up part of the terrain in the battle between Jesus and Satan.

Why is the so-called "secular" worldview positioned as being "politically correct?" Scientism or evolutionism is a worldview that in some cases seeks to replace the Godly worldview. They are worldviews that do not place God at the center of life, let alone Jesus. Do these two worldviews somehow not qualify as being influential? It is an absurdity for me to even consider such a notion. *Of course* scientism and evolutionism are highly influential. So who in the world impresses this upon me, upon us, that scientism or evolutionism or atheism are considered the secular worldviews most suitable for public duty and public places, while Christianity is not? Since when is it wrong or inappropriate to acknowledge reality—I would think honoring God is healthy. It seems simple enough to me that no matter someone's worldview we are all equally influenced by our worldview. Some may be more passionate and vocal and some more secret, but your worldview guides you as much as my worldview guides me. The question is not whether each person has a worldview. The real question is: where does our worldview lead us, and where is it leading others?

The evidence about God puts me in this situation—the situation of being challenged about whom I understand God to be and who God calls me to be, through the Holy Bible. In light of my situation I need to simply address it. By identifying the strife between worldviews I hope to find resolution. But for resolution to come we must all acknowledge reality. So it's only fair and honest we start off admitting we all have a worldview, and that you are using yours and I am using mine. This is realistic. The fear is valid that a nation would compel its citizens to worship God if we choose to acknowledge the reality of God—it does happen. But even God gives us freedom to choose or deny God. No one on earth should think we have the authority to force a person to think, or to love a certain way. Liberty is a principal of God and should be honored by all. I want to see freedom and liberty pursued, while guarding against tyranny. I want to be someone contributing to a cultural system of governance that promotes truth, peace, and the health and well-being of its people. No government is truly able to coerce the heart of a person and should never attempt it. This is very important to understand as the implication of God's message upon Half Dome is sorted out.

My relationship with God compels me to figure out how to live culturally amidst the worldview tensions. If I avoid engaging this issue I then allow myself to be tossed to and fro by forces pulling me away from my relationship with God. I think it's fair to say we all want much of the same things no matter what worldview we hold. We also shouldn't pretend this has nothing to do with the way we govern ourselves as a country—it has everything to do with it. I think many resist acknowledging this for fear that the State would end up mandating religion and there would be no choice. This is a valid concern. Religion or the worship of God should not be mandated or forced. With freedom and liberty comes the obligation and responsibility to preserve freedom itself, to cultivate it and respect it. We can only have liberty by risking liberty. Freedom to worship God exists as long as we are willing to allow freedom from worshipping God. This partnership assures me that at the end of the day it's all right to admit there *is* no principled way to separate our worldview from the way we think, the decisions we make, and the influence we have. It's just a factor of interaction. It's our choice to battle or make peace with each other.

The Dragon Makes War

The hostility between Jesus and the beast portrayed on Half Dome commands my attention. I can't escape it. God is illustrating this reality before our very eyes. I am called back to understand this battle that is so front and center. Can true peace in our world be achieved? Who would be making war if everyone was pursuing peace with one another? Where does war originate? It is written in the Book of Revelation that, "…there was war in heaven, Michael and his angels waging war with the dragon. The dragon and his angels waged war" (Revelation 12:7). This battle was in defense of those the dragon wanted to devour, and "…the dragon was enraged…and went off to make war…[with those] who keep the commandments of God and hold to the testimony of Jesus" (Revelation 12:17). "…The beast that comes up out of the abyss will make war…" (Revelation 11:7).

Jesus said, "He who is not with Me is against Me; and he who does not gather with Me, scatters" (Luke 11:23). His disciple accounted, "[T]he one who practices sin is of the devil; for the devil has sinned from the beginning. [Jesus,] The Son of God appeared for this purpose, to destroy the works of the devil" (1 John 3:8). This great half dome of granite simply illustrates God opposing the devil. It is a reminder that there are two sides to choose from. The right choice seems obvious. At this point, whatever control Satan has is the control surrendered to him. The devil, in fact, has lost the authority over the earth and claim on our souls because Jesus took it back through His death on the cross and resurrection to life.

Knowingly or unknowingly, I've been serving something or someone with my actions, with my money, and with public allegiance. The question is, "who is my master?" Jesus said, "No servant can serve two masters; for either he will hate the one and love the other, or else he will be devoted to one and despise the other…" (Luke 16:13). If not dedicated to God and His purpose, to what am I? "…If God is for us, who is against us?" (Romans 8:31). If I am not for God, could I, perhaps be against God? If I am not for the health and well being of my body, I work against it. If not working for the things of God on earth I work against them, tricked into serving Satan who is working to tear down the kingdom of God. Caught in between the battle of God and the devil, I inevitably build up or tear down one or the other with my choices and actions. I've made a conscience decision to "…choose…today whom [I] will serve…" (Joshua 24:15), and I choose Christ.

"Why are the nations in an uproar And the peoples devising a vain thing?" (Psalm 2:1). I see the rage and greed of this world as the motivation behind the strife and vanity, driving infectious rebellion and terrible war machines. Does war oppress or liberate? The oppressed may see war as a just cause because they are rescued from the oppressor, hoping in turn for freedom. The oppressor wages war for selfish gain at the sake of those he oppresses, placing bondage upon all who threaten his control. Does war become a just cause to punish the oppressor for taking freedom and life away initially? But no matter the reason, war is tragic. Therefore I ask, is war acceptable to God and what do I do about my own country that goes to war with another?

So what do we do with war? I find instruction to, "Never pay back evil for evil to anyone. Respect what is right in the sight of all men. If possible, so far as it depends on you, be at peace with all men. Never take your own revenge…but leave room for the wrath *of God*, for it is written, 'VENGEANCE IS MINE, I WILL REPAY,' says the Lord…Do not be overcome by evil, but overcome evil with good" (Romans 12:17-19, 21). I read how to become equipped and, "Put on the full armor of God, so that you will be able to stand firm against the schemes of the devil…and having done everything, to stand firm" (Ephesians 6:11, 13). If I take a stand for truth, refraining from revenge, seeking peace with all people and overcoming evil with good, who is then making war, and why? Who is the culprit of war?

The angels of God went to war with the dragon to defend the witnesses of Jesus. The motive of the angels was to preserve life and subdue the threat. Throughout the ages of time all peoples and nations have been guilty of going to war for unjust reasons, who've also attempted to argue and rationalize their behavior for war. I reason that if everyone simply stood firm for truth and justice, war is ultimately prevented. Who then has reason to make war? Remaining would only be those who seek the destruction of truth and justice, staking unfair claims, and in fact instigating war. Who's not tired of war? Who doesn't want to live in peace? I know I do and I want others to who are being trod under the feet of constant threat. On the one hand I don't want to ever see another war, and on the other I don't want to see another person oppressed.

Maybe we're not doing a good enough job of holding leaders accountable for engaging in war. The burden ultimately falls on the citizenry to collectively hold the nation of our home accountable to prevent or stop itself from violating other nations and peoples. The people also have the responsibility to keep themselves from being oppressed, which I think starts by honoring the principles and reality of God in Christ. It is through Christ that liberation is given. Unfortunately history is wrought with war and destruction, and war is terrible no matter the reason. The choice exists to stand for and build a nation who honors God, who honors liberty and justice, and chooses to only defend.

We the people have the God-given responsibility to empower leaders who seek the heart of God through deed and not only with words. Any individual appointed to lead should desire the things God desires. Otherwise who is leading us and where are we being led? The real debate should be about what exactly God desires and how we as a people will fulfill them. We shouldn't be afraid to go here, because if we won't truly get to the bottom of *why* our problems exist and *how* God has designed things to work we will never fix what is broken. We will only forever engage in superficial repairs. I also don't see that God has given us authority to give up on trying to resolve our issues and fall back on the "end of the world" either. This tells me that we still need to employ good stewardship of the earthly realm and put people in charge of regions who are faithful to fulfill the principles of God. Any other direction is certain to end up in human oppression to one degree or another. Freedom from personal and societal dysfunction is the vital aim, which I trust is ultimately how war will be prevented, the environment preserved, and people helped. Perhaps it's this simple.

I've got to believe that those who are unable to defend themselves against unprovoked acts of aggression should be defended where possible. It seems that any person or nation who wishes to engage in the oppression of others would be *guilty* of instigating war. Has being evil become a right? It certainly isn't in God's eyes—it's the root problem. The Bible encourages us to let our grievances be known and to ultimately pursue peace. This world is equally ours to make it everything God desires. We are stewards of the earth who've been put in place by God. I want to see peace prevail. This means unity is key. I know I'm being very simplistic on the topic of war and the complexities of war run far, far deeper than

I'm able to address here. But perhaps a more simplistic approach to resolving the issues of war would keep us from engaging in it in the first place. After all, the cultural terrain is determined by the individual perspectives of people at the most basic levels of society. Half Dome illustrates the war between Satan and God. The Bible articulates how war started in the heart of Satan. Now we have the choice as to whom we stand with, and whether or not we let the spirit of war grow within our own hearts. Peace ultimately comes through Christ.

Deception's Control

This sign upon Half Dome is helping to peel the blindness from within me. It has led me to study the Bible in order to make sense of this granite message. I have been summoned to figure out what our reality consists of. A man of Jesus' time once testified that Jesus healed his physical blindness. Since birth he could not see, and then testifying before the religious council that sought to condemn Jesus to death he stated, "…though I was blind, now I see" (John 9:25). When you read the story you get the sense that this is all the man knew about Jesus, and that nothing else really mattered. This was his report to the council. In the spiritual sense Jesus is healing the blindness of my own heart and mind. With sight being restored in me I now assemble my wits to navigate through the battle between good and evil. The clash on Half Dome gets right to the point—the beast seeks to devour. I am to be on the lookout for the tactics of the devil. Its snarl and salivating mouth tell me so.

If evil has a hope I would guess it to be the gain of ultimate power over God to oppress God's creation. Satan is working to achieve this goal through the force of deception. Perhaps this is Satan's only hope to escape the judgment of God and lead others to believe the same. Jesus said this of the devil: "…He was a murderer from the beginning, and does not stand in the truth because there is no truth in him…for he is a liar and the father of lies" (John 8:44). The words of Jesus written by His disciples reveal Satan's nature. It is also written that, "…Satan disguises himself as an angel of light" (2 Corinthians 11:14) and goes on to say, "Therefore it is not surprising if his servants also disguise themselves as servants of righteousness…"

(2 Corinthians 11:15). Satan does not work alone in his deceptions. He employs his fallen angels and maybe even some of us by misleading all who fall victim to his lies. Evil forces depend on our mind being closed to truth and knowledge in order to perpetrate evil acts. There exists this whole other realm working intensely to destroy what is good and what is alive.

It's therefore critical I remain open to learning what is true, or evil will take advantage of me. Even though the identity of God is clear, there is still much to learn about the nature of God. I can't afford obstacles of arrogance, stubbornness or ignorance to build up within me. They block my ability to live as God intends. If I don't acknowledge the battle happening within or around me I am deceived. Obstacles of self-pride and apathy work to beat down Godly humility and awareness. If I choose to cultivate these obstacles (my way over God's way; seeking the high esteem of others over doing what is right; wanting revenge; holding grudges; a poor self image; etc.), as being acceptable to God, I then live according to lies. Thinking God does not exist is an obstacle. Telling myself God does not exist because I don't want to go to church, or be religious, or that the devil is pretend, or do things I know I shouldn't be doing, builds up these obstacles. I then somehow feel more and more justified to build my life around them. If I allow myself to avoid resolving the problems within me, in turn I push myself away from God out of guilt or spiritual blindness. I end up allowing the obstacles and barriers in my life to set up permanent residence. The more I do this the more closed off to God I become.

According to the nature of Satan, this is where the beast wants me—trapped within my own mind, unwilling or unable to see truth. The reason why I get trapped is irrelevant. I'm simply trapped. What matters to Satan is that I'm closed to knowing the truth about myself, about others, about reality, and God. If the devil and his angels trick me into believing he is not real or that God does not exist, or perhaps that God is some other god, his lies succeed and destruction prevails.

Breaking A Spell

When I look out into the broad landscape of the world I see masses of people believing in God, yet in different and contradicting natures of God. And out of these masses I see many having a double-principled mindset: possessing a non-literal view of religion or spirituality, with the underlying goal of sanctioning opposing core principles of God, or better yet, overlooking them in the name of diversity. Simply stated: believing one thing while at the same time acting contrary to that belief. I wonder to what degree I possess a double-principled mindset without even knowing it? I feel God leading me to analyze this predicament, because this state of mind is yet another major front in the battle over our souls between God and the devil. This is the kind of pitfall that stirs me deeply. I want to help free the captive.

Unfortunately, many of us get drawn into this trap in many different ways. Perhaps it's a result of the misunderstanding people have about subjective and objective truth—unsure about the relationship of mind and matter and how they practically meet in reality. I see this way of thinking being further exacerbated when the spiritual soul is thought of as being disconnected from the physical body—reasoning reality is two, unrelated parts: spirit and matter, or that spirit is good and matter is evil. I learned that this way of thinking is primarily Greek-based, dating way back—perhaps unconsciously designed to pretend there is no problem with "believing in God," while at the same time being hedonistic—knowingly or unknowingly.

Thinking and living this way serves to trick me into believing my actions are separate from what I believe spiritually. Proverbs 23:7 says that whatever a person thinks within, that is who they really are. Believing my actions don't need to be or aren't connected to my spiritual worldview would diagnose an infection of a "double-principled mindset." This is can also be referred to as dualism. I lack integrity and reliability when I possess this dualistic mindset. It's even possible for an entire culture to be this way.

A good example of dualistic thinking is, "Do as I say, not as I do." It's one thing to make unhealthy choices or grave mistakes, acknowledge them, and move to reconcile. It's dualistic to fool myself to think I'm not making unhealthy choices or grave mistakes, while simultaneously condemning the very acts I unabashedly engage in. The Book of James writes that, "...a double-minded man [is] unstable in all his ways" (James 1:8). I don't want to be unstable. The whole reason for my search is to gain stability by knowing God through the truth. I've got to make sure

I weed out this kind of dysfunction in my life. These are the roots of hypocrisy. So in regards to taking oaths (or making promises) the Bible says to "…let your statement be, 'Yes, yes' *or* 'No, no'; anything beyond these is of evil" (Matthew 5:37).

The point made in both verses of James and Matthew is for me to simply speak and live the truth—say what I mean and mean what I say; do what I say and say what I do. This sounds so basic. I feel like I've climbed a mountain of information for a revelation confirming the same common sense many of us already have. But confirmation is good, especially from God. It's clear we are expected by God to stand firm on these principles without worrying that someone else may be offended when we do. Of course in being bold I need to employ thoughtfulness and respect with each situation and person. I don't have license from God to go around offending others. Loving my neighbor as myself will help remind me to communicate with others in the way I'd like to be communicated with. So in respectful and loving ways we've got to help hold each other to what we say and do. Otherwise we enable dualism, and foster hypocrisy.

When we individually or as a culture rebuke the very acts we in actuality engage in we commit a form of evil. This is according to Jesus, because "anything beyond this is of evil." These are His words. Ground is taken away from us when we play into Satan's hands through this "double standard," creating unrest and dysfunction within our soul and between our fellow human being. This turns people off and away from truth. Apathy spreads like disease. Strife begins taking shape. Tension and anger build tabernacles of discontentment that produce the plots of rage, potentially manifesting into violence and ultimately war. I see broken promises and injustice as being key reasons our world rages with itself. God's word tells me, "…in all things show yourself to be an example of good deeds…" (Titus 2:7). It is clear that God is directing me to do "good." And before I knew Jesus, God through my conscience was leading me in this same direction.

I know this sounds so elementary and hearing me say this makes me think, "How else would I expect life to be?" But when I look around I see people who passionately profess to know God while at the same time engaging in evil acts—on a global scale and even in personal situations reported through the media. Maybe it's just a case of easier said than done, but still, there's no valid excuse here. I see dualism often wounding many people emotionally through sexual behavior. More and more I'm frustrated to see our culture verbally communicating to children that abstaining from sexual intercourse until marriage is safe and healthy while saying, "But if you're going to have sex be smart. Use birth control and protect yourself from disease." The first part of this message aligns with what God commands. The second part is what God calls evil, because I don't find any principles of God that endorse premarital sex. But among adults premarital sex is promoted as being cool and acceptable, while virginity and fidelity are chided at many turns through common social interactions and large-scale media. This has got to be one of the most striking examples of dualism, producing very destructive results. Both men and women are cheapened and hurt emotionally when *used* sexually. This is one major way the battle between good and evil manifests itself into our physical world.

I also see a vicious cycle: men and boys lusting after women and girls; girls and women giving in sexually to them with hopes of being accepted and loved—in some cases out of fear. And then the girl ends up hurt and jaded because his sexual desires were fulfilled; he then ends whatever relationship had been started, which he likely never intended to keep to begin with. She is left to feel exploited, rejected, and ends up used. He falsely justifies his motives in hopes of preventing the guilt of his selfish acts. I know I'm painting in broad strokes here and I know there is much more to it than this. But this is a common situation, and for some a common strategy. Sexual pressure is a very real and destructive social situation and evil lurks to take advantage of our insecurities here.

I know deep down, my conscience communicates sex is something sacred and meant for marriage. You probably feel the same. But the culture and peer pressure seem to make fun of those who want to wait for sex until married, or not have sex at all. Intense pressure is applied, tricking us to believe we should be having promiscuous, unmarried sexual intercourse in order to be or feel accepted. It's like I'm made to think there is something wrong with me if I choose not to have sex, when in fact, I'm starting to understand that it's perfectly right to feel this way—that it's healthy and good to want to abstain sexually until married.

The problem is further exacerbated when the majority of a culture promotes sexual promiscuity, sanctioning what we struggle to discipline. Instead of stopping the promiscuous behavior significantly causing problems in our children, parts of our culture attempt to facilitate some sort of safe sexual intercourse—believing there is no worthy alternative. This dualism allows us to essentially give up and refuse to stop the obvious contributor: our own sexual hypocrisy and selfishness as adults. I believe this is dualism at its finest accoding to the principles of darkness—at one of its worst according to the priciples of God.

You and I are at the center of this struggle. We battle growing up in life to do what we think will help us. When I am more afraid of Satan's name-calling and emotional or physical abuse over God's judgment and wrath for my own sin, the devil is in control of me. Even though we know we ultimately want our life to be with God we can find ourselves pushed away from God in this situation.

The greatest deception Satan perpetrates through dualism is with the nature of truth. Somehow, people and cultures come to feel, assume, or hope that conflicting or opposing claims, notions, or theories can simultaneously be true. How is it possible that God almighty exists to many people, while to others, God is a figment of imagination? Or that God can be one God and many different gods, or be animals or trees? I'm so tired and worn out from things not making sense! I set out on a quest for the objective truth about God in hopes of settling this matter once and for all.

How much oppression and suffering in the world is a result of the profound denial of truth and justice? The whole point to my search was to gain powerful resolution and base my life upon the truth about God—the natural law. Frustration has gnawed at me whenever I've come up to conflicting truths because people tell me it's all right; this is just the way things are. *How* are things—that the world is just messed up or that we can all have our own individual truth, regardless of whether it's even true? This is not logical, much less possible. But nevertheless, I'm told not to bother with trying to resolve it.

As a result, the world collectively concludes that it's better to accept everything and avoid educating ourselves about what's actually true. These are good intentions, but how much false reality is being taught for the illusion of unity? What do we think the result will be? This is a path of inevitable deception led by a beast the world will one day see. Avoiding reality in the name of unity does not lead to unity, but apathy, disaffection, and destruction. I'm under the spell of dualism if I think otherwise.

Each person makes up their culture in which we live, shaping it, making positive contributions, or negatively draining life. Is anyone exempt? Every message, advertisement, movie, art form, or image we put out influences thoughts and actions. People advertise their worldview with words, lifestyle, and actions. Corporations advertise with billboards, commercials, and product placement. What we consume and support says who we are. What we feed grows.

Are we the kind of people who don't want children to smoke, but smoke anyway? Are we fathers who don't want our daughters being taken advantage of sexually, but support pornography or sexual promiscuity? Do we complain about the way our government runs the nation, yet do not voice our opinion, or vote if able to? Do we claim to follow God, yet discard Godly principles we don't agree with or find offensive to our lifestyle?

We've got a big battle to fight against the dualism in our brain. Its common hold runs havoc, in turn gripping our culture and scheduling the next generations to become more and more disillusioned. We have the opportunity to inspire the young to live more meaningfully, to achieve that which we were not able or ready to achieve. I think we miss opportunities to truly know God, to pass on an eternal, healthy legacy. As a world and culture, we're not reaching the fullest potential possible. We can choose to do something about it.

Why should I wait until faced with death to come to terms with God and miss out on living a full life? A relationship with God has got to be the greatest opportunity! Who knows my last day, but God? A life of meaning and principle is ready to be claimed and lived, which is all the more reason to understand just how much my disorientation has kept me from a purpose-filled life. I call on God to awake my mind and spirit—to reveal truth and eradicate confusion.

The Issue of Morality

With the reality of God reaching through Half Dome, ultimate moral authority is resting on Jesus because of what is written in the Bible about Him. This marks one of the most intense matters on the battleground. Cultures and parts of cultures clash over moral authority. People clash. Lives get broken. This issue stood between Jesus and me as a line in the sand. Part of me resisted obedience to God, while part of me didn't understand the forgiveness of God. But once I realized that Jesus is God I became compelled to examine my actions in light of Biblical morality. In turn I took responsibility to begin examining the cultural issues of our day in light of the Bible. Identifying the Bible's position in regards to morality was much simpler than I thought it would be, though being introduced to the highest standards proves challenging. Fortunately (or unfortunately depending on how you look at it) things are specifically laid out about how God intends us to live. It's becoming clear about how I hurt myself emotionally or otherwise. One of the places I started was with the Ten Commandments.

The Ten Commandments:

One: "You shall have no other gods before Me" (Exodus 20:3).

Two: "You shall not make for yourself an idol, or any likeness of what it is in heaven above or on the earth beneath or in the water under the earth. You shall not worship them or serve them…" (Exodus 20:4-5).

Three: "You shall not take the name of the LORD your God in vain…" (Exodus 20:7).

Four: "Remember the Sabbath day, to keep it holy" (Exodus 20:8).

Five: "Honor your father and mother…" (Exodus 20:12).

Six: "You shall not murder" (Exodus 20:13).

Seven: "You shall not commit adultery" (Exodus 20:14).

Eight: "You shall not steal" (Exodus 20:15).

Nine: "You shall not bear false witness against your neighbor" (Exodus 20:16).

Ten: "You shall not covet…anything that belongs to your neighbor" (Exodus 20:17).

This seems pretty straight and forward. I'd like to further clarify a couple of commandments, but how can I argue with this tangible list? I don't see how anything here could be categorized as being negative or bad. I think the Sabbath Day refers to having a day of rest in a week. I'll take it! The Sabbath also has something to do going to going to church. I don't know exactly what it means to take the Lord's name in vain, but I would agree that cursing the name of Jesus or God and having a worthless attitude about God would not be something positive. The rest of the Ten Commandments are very clear and concisely make their point.

Jesus spoke of two commandments, clarifying that, "...YOU SHALL LOVE THE LORD YOUR GOD WITH ALL YOUR HEART, AND WITH ALL YOUR SOUL, AND WITH ALL YOUR MIND, AND WITH ALL YOUR STRENGTH. The second is this, 'YOU SHALL LOVE YOUR NEIGHBOR AS YOURSELF.' There is no other commandment greater than these" (Mark 12:31).

Not only did Jesus speak of these two commandments, He said they were the greatest ones. This makes absolute sense that God should come first. God is life. Without life what is there? Nothing. And it feels good to hear that loving others is the next greatest virtue to loving God. When I think of these two commandments together I think of peace. Life would truly be different when lived according to what Jesus commands here. It almost sounds too simple. Maybe it's because I think things are more complicated when perhaps they're really not. What's to argue here about these Biblical commandments? I see them as being very constructive and helpful instructions.

However, there are battles both within the soul and in conversations taking place in the public discourse over more provocative morals found in passages such as this:

"For the wrath of God is revealed from heaven against all ungodliness and unrighteousness of men who suppress the truth in unrighteousness... Therefore God gave them over in the lusts of their hearts to impurity...to degrading passions...women exchanged the natural function for that which is unnatural, and in the same way also the men abandoned the natural function of the woman and burned in their desire toward one another, men with men committing indecent acts...And just as they did not see fit to acknowledge God any longer, God gave them over to a depraved mind, to do those things which are not proper" (Romans 1:18, 24, 26-28).

"For this is the will of God, your sanctification; *that is*, that you abstain from sexual immorality" (1 Thessalonians 4:3).

The battle is fierce over sexual conduct. Sexual desires, predilections, weaknesses, and Godly natural design make for great controversy and conflict about this matter. Those who believe in "anything goes" resist the morality of God expressed through the Bible. Those who align with the morality of God confront those to be considered rebelling. Even in between both sides there's some who secretly resent their sexuality or morality, yet struggle to be obedient for acceptance or fear of God or people. Sexuality can be profoundly complex. It seems obvious that out of all the things in this world we desire or struggle with, for most people it is sex.

I know I desire to be sexual with a woman, but I've been afraid of marriage because I see so many of them broken and failed. It's been impressed in my mind that if I want to be sexual with a woman and she with me then we need to marry for sexual intercourse to be right in the eyes of God. Otherwise, I would be committing sexual immorality. But what if I love that person and choose to be with her only? Is it still immoral if we choose not to marry? What makes sex immoral inside of a loving relationship who are not legally married? Isn't it love that matters most? Jesus referred to marriage this way:

Have you not read that He who created them from the beginning, MADE THEM MALE AND FEMALE, and said, 'FOR THIS REASON A MAN SHALL LEAVE HIS FATHER AND MOTHER AND BE JOINED TO HIS WIFE, AND THE TWO SHALL BECOME ONE FLESH?' So they are no longer two, but one flesh. What therefore God has joined together, let no man separate (Matthew 19:4-6).

And the standard of God rises even higher when Jesus says in the same conversation, "And I say to you, whoever divorces his wife, except for immorality, and marries another woman commits adultery" (Matthew 19:9). Jesus also said this about adultery: "You have heard that it was said, 'YOU SHALL NOT COMMIT ADULTERY'; but I say to you that everyone who looks…with lust…has already committed adultery…in his heart" (Matthew 5:27-28). There's no doubt that God is setting the bar at the highest level in regards to the fidelity between a man and woman. When looking with lust is considered adultery in the eyes of God we know we're faced with the highest sexual standard. It seems so unrealistic, and maybe from our perspective it is, but I'm now called to see things the way God does because Christ is in me. And thank God because there is no doubt I've committed sin.

The Apostle Paul weighs by writing in 1 Corinthians 7:9, "…for it is better to marry than to burn *with passion*." Hebrews 13:4 says that, "Marriage *is to be held* in honor among all, and the marriage bed is to be undefiled; for fornicators and adulterers God will judge." Cleary sex outside of marriage is being looked down upon here. Who is not challenged here to do what is right in the eyes of God? Everyone is challenged! But at the same time, much of the world and culture today thinks this is foolishness. "Have sex if you want, just be 'smart' about it," parts of the culture say. But the Bible is telling me that the physical relationship between a man and a woman is sacred. I can't seem to find anything in the Bible that permits sexual intercourse outside of marriage, or between anyone other than one man and one woman.

These standards seem almost impossible to live up to! And it's all the more discouraging when sexual images are all around—television, the internet, advertising, etc. "Sex sells, so sell it!" is the strategy of Satan to draw me into failure, coaxing me to give in and commit sexual immorality in the eyes of God. As a result, sexual connotations end up everywhere—even in children's cartoons, comic books, and graphic novels. Who is not bombarded with sexual images these days? The sexual battleground for our mind and soul is vicious. Satan's tactics are almost overwhelming. Self-resolution says, "Give in. Resistance is futile!"

I have to remind myself in all of this that Jesus is saying it's sinful to look upon another person with lust. It's hard to fathom that God considers thinking lustful thoughts to be adultery of the heart, but God's ways are the highest. Since I understand actions are birthed out of thought, how can I logically argue that impure and unhealthy ideas won't lead to sinful and unhealthy acts? They almost always do. My flesh fights for its own desires while my spirit wants to do the right thing. This is a major area of struggle for so many of us. The devil hits us hard here. To do what is right doesn't seem so easy. But Jesus opposes the beast and because I stand with Jesus, I too can stand against the devil.

Maybe God's standards seem almost unrealistic, but I've got to trust God that this is the way I should go. If I can't trust God, who then? I can't say I want to quickly agree and give up doing things that seem pleasing to me and not pleasing to God, but I must come to terms with reality. The Bible makes it clear, "...Do not be deceived; neither fornicators, nor idolaters, nor adulterers, nor effeminate, nor homosexuals, nor thieves, nor *the* covetous, nor drunkards, nor revilers, nor swindlers, will inherit the kingdom of God" (1 Corinthians 6:9-10).

Who is left after this; certainly no one who has ever done anything wrong? Fortunately the Bible doesn't leave me hanging here. It goes on to say, "Such were some of you; but you were washed, but you were sanctified, but you were justified in the name of the Lord Jesus Christ and in the Spirit of our God" (1 Corinthians 6:11). I may not fully understand being washed, and sanctified, and justified, but the more I understand the battle over my soul, the more I realize trust in Christ, as Savior, is how to win. Jesus even forgives me for what I've done.

The best I can do is keep trying, never giving up, and realize I am prone to fail because of my sin and dysfunction. I can see how easily discouraged I may become following God, trying to live up to the highest standards. But what is the alternative? I see it two ways: either I can stand with Jesus and not see this as being a miserable set of rules telling me what *not* to do, but rather seeing it as a great opportunity to discover new life; all the while knowing that Jesus walks with me as my strength. Or I'm on the side of the beast, fulfilling his ways. Either way, I will battle and contend for the ground I claim. Why should I not battle on the side of Jesus instead of fighting alone, manipulated by evil, against God?

I don't think life is just about avoiding sin either and trying *not* to mess up. I think it's really about taking a stand, living for God, and being conscience of the war between good and evil in the battle over my soul. And in battle victory is possible, which means there is hope. It is written in Romans that if God is for us, who can be against us. I realize my mind and spirit must be constantly awakened to the surrounding reality. By better understanding this intense battle, I will better know how to live victoriously for God and with God. Fortunately the Bible *teaches* victory in God, but if I'm under the spell of evil spiritual obstacles will prevail within me. My desire is to see and walk in obedience to God. Lord help me!

Chapter Five

Common Ground

"Science is not threatened by God; it is enhanced.
God is most certainly not threatened by science; He made it all possible.
So let us together seek to reclaim the solid ground
of an intellectually and spiritually satisfying synthesis of all great truths.
That ancient motherland of reason and worship
was never in danger of crumbling.
It never will be.
It beckons all sincere seekers of truth
to come and take up residence there."
– Francis S. Collins

It has been about a year since my first visit to Yosemite in 1992. Since last spring I've been working diligently to reconcile what these images of Half Dome represent and in large part I am. I've also tuned in to the public discourse in the television media and dialogue over the airwaves of radio. I hear the battle over what's true and right taking place before my very ears. I perceive the sounds of our true common ground presenting itself, while simultaneously hearing them being trampled by misunderstandings and deceptions and then brought back to reality by another—back and forth. The first stirrings of wanting to engage in the cultural conversation begin to take hold in me. I sense this sign from God on Half Dome will answer some of the biggest questions people have. I believe the solid ground of truth is something able to be clearly articulated for our world to grasp. I'm now engrossed in the process of sorting out this sign from God and what's happening in the world, as well as personally in my own life. My mission in life feels as though it is being awakened. I have the strange feeling like it was always within me, just dormant.

I feel bombarded with information! And it's no wonder—I sought it all out.

I'm glad though, because much is becoming clear about reality and who God is and who we are on this journey called life. Still, my brain and spirit need respite. I can't think of a better place to get away to than the supernatural valley that inspires me. It's time to get out and go revisit the wilderness that God is also speaking to me through. Now that winter has come and gone I want to return once again and encounter the valley that God is using to change my heart and mind.

My Gramma had given me a couple of old backpacks she got from a thrift store because she thought I might want to go hiking—just out of the blue. Maybe I said something to tip her off. I don't know, but if you knew my Gramma you'd know she has a way about her that's quite peculiar. Without going into much detail, let's just say her gift was tuning into a person's life to meet their needs. It was somewhat strange but she usually was able to fill distinctive needs with little information. A specific example is with my brother Adam. Before he was born my Gramma started preparing for special medical needs. None of it made any sense until he was born with cerebral palsy. It's not that she necessarily was gathering things she would be able to use to care for him. It was more her mindset or her spirit preparing. She ended up helping my parents care for him five days a week until he was too big for her to handle. My Gramma exemplified the heart of God through her sacrificial love given to our family. And now that my walk with the Lord is becoming more and more practical each day, I see God's hand working through so many different facets of life—even through my Gramma's insightful ways.

So I graciously accepted her gift of these two used backpacks. I took the best of each to make one good one. I get my map of Yosemite and start planning my trip. This time I plan to see Half Dome as close up as possible. Looking at the map, North Dome seems to put me about three thousand feet up into the air, directly across from the face of Half Dome. So that's my destination for my solo mission. I look forward to being alone to hear from God if God would have anything to say to me in whatever way. I wonder if there will be anything new to gather? Maybe not, but at the very least I hope to come away with more pictures and unwind amidst all the research, study, and intense discussions within the public discourse I am now beginning to engage—at least in thought.

Once in Yosemite Valley with my hiking permit in hand, I park my Jeep by Mirror Lake to catch the trailhead to North Dome. Things start off pretty well. I feel good and very excited to get up there. I'm looking at about a six or seven-mile hike and plan to spend the night there somewhere. I'm in decent shape and anticipate the hike to be pretty moderate. This was my first backpack trip ever and the first time to put on about forty pounds of gear to set out to somewhere in the wilderness I had not been. And as I start hiking the steep switchbacks I realize this is far from a walk in the park. My brisk pace turns to an out of breath walk and the weight of my pack is starting to dig into my shoulders. I begin trying to relieve the pressure of the pack's shoulder straps digging into me, pulling up the bottom of the aluminum frame with my hands, but only to have my arms tire. After a couple hours of the back and forth pain of my shoulders and arms I realize what that waist belt was for—that thing I didn't think I needed back at home for some foolish reason. What was I thinking! "What a rookie," I think to myself—beyond rookie, really.

Now what do I do? I'm thinking I'm about half way or so up this three thousand plus vertical rise and it will level out soon and I'll be there. I don't want to turn back. I've come this far and the most difficult part is almost over. I'll just keep walking—and walking, and walking, and walking. Then spots on the ground along the trail start to look mighty good for setting up for the night. But no! I've set out to make it to North Dome! "Just keep going!" I tell myself. "This is just a hike. No this is ridiculous!" I came to unwind but now I'm all twisted up and tired. I reckon that the wilderness is certainly nothing to mess with.

I eventually get to North Dome, but with only enough time to take a quick look at Half Dome before the sun faded and the landscape was covered with darkness. And you could only imagine about all the other little things I didn't plan out very well—like having enough water! But the night turned out to be awesome. As soon as the summer dusk winds settled down from the afternoon heat rising off the valley floor, the stars showed as though I was on the moon. Almost one hundred and eighty degrees of star-lit space surrounded me, and right across the deep valley I had just hiked up, stood the silhouette of Half Dome set off by the infinite number of stars behind it. Even though the darkness enveloped me I felt the presence of God in this surreal setting. I felt the peace of God within me. This moment felt very special, and I started longing for someone to share it with. So as a single man, I felt compelled to take the opportunity to pray to God for my future wife whom I did not yet know. I prayed for God to be with her until we meet, and that she and I would be able to share this heavenly moment atop this great valley together some day.

As I continued looking into the endless atmosphere at the infinite number of stars, I thought about the countless number of people in the world. Just contemplating the multitudes and multitudes of people alive right now on this planet amazed me. There are so many people going about their day or sleeping, yet under the same heaven, with the same God watching over. I remember turning to look intently at the shape of Half Dome through the darkness thinking that this rock wall is something we all physically have in common. This very terra firma is common ground we tread with our feet. I was reminded that in a vast sea of diversity and uncertainties exists great clarity by way of the truth. I sense God is connecting us to each other through the truth, which hits home that we truly do have vitally shared common ground.

I took away from my outing that Half Dome indeed stands as a common landmark to millions and millions, and the deep, deep answers of its face are revealing God as our origin—the common ground we share. Fibers of truth bind us. Even our genetic code confirms a common, physical foundation. Yet throughout my life I've worked so hard to become individualized, resisting the common mold. Did I do this just for the sake of being different from the next person? In part I think I was resisting Jesus in order to save my own individuality. I assumed being a Christian meant perhaps casting away my personal goals and dreams to never realize them. But if I let the tactics of Satan lead me away from Jesus in order to stand out as an "isolated individual," what really have I achieved? Satan would succeed in separating me from God.

Reaching common ground starts with the individual—with me, and with you. It starts with identifying what's most vital to us. I want to look at what the wrath of God is all about. It would be constructive to understand how fear fits into this equation. I hope to fully grasp His justice and mercy. Perhaps in gaining wisdom about these central aspects we might find the bridge to greater common ground. I know we have many of the same fears, but also many of the same hopes. It's just a matter of identifying them.

Just how difficult is it for us to commit to the common ground of Jesus? It's more and more obvious to me that God is making Jesus the focus. Maybe we hesitate because God poses to change our life in ways we don't think we want Him to. But what's worth holding on to that we'd sacrifice eternal life for? I can't think of anything more important than being alive. God has been asking me to trust in Jesus to save me from wrath and judgment, so there is nothing to hesitate about or be afraid of. If I can't trust God, whom then can I trust? Who else but God gives life? So trusting in Jesus makes perfect, logical sense, but by resisting what's true a "whole" world is not able to form. We remain somewhat disjointed as a community.

Maybe we let what others think get in the way. Some people think that trust in Jesus as a Savior is nonsense—"Being saved from what?" is the response. Others hope that everyone who is "good" will go to heaven to be with God without needing to trust in Jesus. But how do they know for sure? This is too big a deal to go just on feelings or hope—it's got to be evident. The whole point to my search has been to know the truth for certain. We've got to be sure about this. In the end, who will be standing with me before God to answer? According to everything I'm finding—no one but Jesus. The common ground of our very heart and soul then is revealed as Christ.

The record about Jesus is historically sound, and provable as having occurred. History does not dispute that Jesus was here, and walked this earth, and that he was crucified. There also has never been a reasonable explanation from the Roman or Jewish authorities as to what happened to His body after He was laid to rest in a Roman-guarded tomb. The only valid reason making sense is that Christ *did* rise from the dead, and was witnessed by His disciples who themselves were eventually put to death for proclaiming Jesus as the risen Savior. It's been recorded that many others also saw Jesus after His resurrection before He was witnessed ascending into the sky. This is an observation of facts about the reality we all share.

Our common ground says God created us and the heavens and the earth. Our commonality says all people have disobeyed God and justice will punish us because of sin. We have in common that Jesus came to set us free from God's wrath against sin if we trust in Jesus. Half Dome and the images upon it are common ground, given by God to better understand the one reality we share. This truth is able to unite us if we so desire.

I've felt the temptation to rebel against this in hopes of creating my own identity, but realize I've already lost my identity to sin. Jesus came to bring a new identity to all who choose to be rooted in Him. He said, "He who has found his life will lose it, and he who has lost his life for My sake will find it" (Matthew 10:39). There's no point in trying to find or assert my individuality at the sake of rejecting God because I'm fearful of losing my identity. If I do I will stay lost. The truth is pointing to the common ground of Christ, which ultimately locates us within reality.

The Wrath of God

The coming judgment of God is something we all share. The anger of God is directed at our world for the sinful things we've done. The presence of darkness in this world is undeniable. When I look at Half Dome I see a dark void between the images of Jesus and the beast. The prophet Jeremiah speaks of a "...deep darkness..." in his book, chapter thirteen, verse sixteen. The words of Jeremiah are interpreted as the shadow of death. We all happen to be situated between good and evil.

I don't want to hang by a thread in the balance awaiting the judgment of God and be ignorant of the foretold wrath against evil. I want to comprehend God's fury and move closer to God into His mercy and forgiveness—a love greater than all. Christ carries the future wrath and judgment in His hand. Both aspects of God are equally real. I need to understand this wrath just as I do His mercy, and in turn perhaps better understand the essence of love. God's anger is something I haven't thought a whole lot about. In the past I knew I loved God and hoped God loved me, and because I've given my heart to Jesus the concern of God's wrath and judgment seem to dramatically fade away. Nonetheless, the coming wrath of God is eminent for which we should be familiar with. We are shown God's opposition to evil on Half Dome and in the Bible, and His furious image is a reality.

When I look at this detailed image of Jesus above, I observe the white of His eye fixed with an intense, blazing stare into the beast. A prophet of old had written, "'So as I live,' declares the LORD GOD, 'surely, because you have defiled My sanctuary with all your detestable idols and with all your abominations, therefore I will also withdraw, and My eye will have no pity and I will not spare'" (Ezekiel 5:11). These words come alive as I witness this remarkable sight of the white of His eye penetrating the beast. It helps to illustrate Ezekiel's point for me.

The most striking feature of this sign is the shout of Christ. This one aspect speaks multitudes! The shout of God is something of great anticipation that marks the return of the Lord, signifying the very end of the world. This image is laced throughout the Bible.

The Bible describes how God shouts against His enemies before He prevails over them: "The Lord will go forth like a warrior, He will arouse *His* zeal like a man of war. He will utter a shout, yes, He will raise a war cry. He will prevail against His enemies" (Isaiah 42:13). The shout signifies warning—God will *shout* before He strikes.

The shout of Jesus upon Half Dome foreshadows the judgment to come: "See to it that you do not refuse Him who is speaking. For if those did not escape when they refused him who warned *them* on earth, much less *will* we *escape* who turn away from Him who *warns* from heaven? And His voice shook the earth then [on Mt. Sinai with Moses, recorded in Exodus 19:18], but now He has promised, saying, 'YET ONCE MORE I WILL SHAKE NOT ONLY THE EARTH, BUT ALSO THE HEAVEN.'...for our God is a consuming fire" (Heb 12:25-26, 29).

The writer of Hebrews is referring back to the days of Moses, at the time when Moses received the Commandments from God on Mt. Sinai: "Now Mt. Sinai *was* all in smoke because the LORD descended upon it in fire; and its smoke ascended like the smoke of a furnace, and the whole mountain quaked violently. When the sound of the trumpet grew louder and louder, Moses spoke and God answered him with thunder" (Exodus 19:18-19).

Over 2,500 years ago, the prophet Jeremiah spoke of things to come when the Jewish people of Israel would be invaded and taken away by the Babylonian kingdom:

"Therefore you shall prophesy against them all these words,

and you shall say to them,

'The LORD will roar from on high

And utter His voice from His holy habitation;

He will roar mightily against His fold.

He will shout like those who tread *the grapes*,

Against all the inhabitants of the earth.

'A clamor has come to the end of the earth,

Because the LORD has a controversy with the nations

He is entering into judgment with all flesh;

(Jeremiah 25:30-31).

This is an intense passage of scripture. The "shout" and "roar" spoken of by the prophet of old is most significant in regards to God's character, the character present upon Half Dome. The "controversy with the nations" mentioned by Jeremiah is this:

> "…For the LORD has a case against the inhabitants of the land, Because there is no faithfulness or kindness Or knowledge of God in the land. *There is* swearing, deception, murder, stealing and adultery. They employ violence, so that bloodshed follows bloodshed. Therefore the land mourns, And everyone who lives in it languishes Along with the beasts of the field and the birds of the sky, And also the fish of the sea disappear" (Hosea 4:1-3).

The Lord's wrath is directed at unfaithfulness, cruelty, personal violations, and sexual immorality. Violence and bloodshed causing the mourning of a people and destroying the environment stirs up the anger of God. The extent of God's wrath extends into the heavens:

> "…YET ONCE MORE I WILL SHAKE NOT ONLY THE EARTH, BUT ALSO THE HEAVEN" (Hebrews 12:26).

There remain tremendous things to come. How could the future hold anything less than our past? The prophecy of the Book of Revelation gives us astonishing imaginary throughout the following verses. From the point of God's judgment accompanied by sounds and peals of thunder to the coming of the new heaven and new earth, this passage of scripture gives a very comprehensive look at how the Apostle John saw the end of the world. The power that will proceed out of the mouth of Christ is described here:

> "…the time *came* for the dead to be judged, and *the time* to reward Your bond-servants the prophets and the saints and those who fear Your name, the small and the great, and to destroy those who destroy the earth. And the temple of

God which is in heaven was opened; and the ark of His covenant appeared in His temple, and there were flashes of lightning and sounds and peals of thunder and an earthquake and a great hailstorm" (Revelation 11:18-19).

"And I saw heaven opened, and behold, a white horse, and He who sat on it *is* called Faithful and True, and in righteousness He judges and wages war. His eyes *are* a flame of fire, and on His head *are* many diadems; and He has a name written *on Him* which no one knows except Himself. *He is* clothed with a robe dipped in blood, and His name is called The Word of God. And the armies which are in heaven, clothed in fine linen, white *and* clean, were following Him on white horses. From His mouth comes a sharp sword, so that with it He may strike down the nations, and He will rule them with a rod of iron; and He treads the wine press of the fierce wrath of God, the Almighty. And on His robe and on His thigh He has a name written, 'KING OF KINGS, AND LORD OF LORDS.' Then I saw an angel standing in the sun, and he cried out with a loud voice, saying to all the birds which fly in midheaven, 'Come, assemble for the great supper of God, so that you may eat the flesh of kings and the flesh of commanders and the flesh of mighty men and the flesh of horses and of those who sit on them and the flesh of all men, both free men and slaves, and small and great.' And I saw the beast and the kings of the earth and their armies assembled to make war against Him who sat on the horse and against His army. And the beast was seized, and with him the false prophet who performed the signs in his presence, by which he deceived those who had received the mark of the beast and those who worshiped his image; these two were thrown alive into the lake of fire which burns with brimstone. And the rest were killed with the sword which came from the mouth of Him who sat on the horse, and all the birds were filled with their flesh" (Revelation 19:11-21).

"Then I saw a great white throne and Him who sat upon it, from whose presence earth and heaven fled away, and no place was found for them. And I saw the dead, the great and the small, standing before the throne, and books were opened; and another book was opened, which is *the book* of life; and the dead were judged from the things which were written in the books, according to their deeds. And the sea gave up the dead which were in it, and death and Hades gave up the dead which were in them; and they were judged, every one *of them* according to their deeds. Then death and Hades were thrown into the lake of fire. This is the second death, the lake of fire. And if anyone's name was not found written in the book of life, he was thrown into the lake of fire…for the cowardly and unbelieving and abominable and murderers and immoral persons and sorcerers and idolaters and all liars, their part *will be* in the lake that burns with fire and brimstone, which is the second death" (Revelation 20:11-15, 21:8).

This is an enormous amount to take in here. I'm barely able to grasp the imagery of this passage as being future events. I'm brought back to the face of Half Dome when I read about the image of Christ being described as having eyes like a flame fire, and out of His mouth He will strike. These words of scripture are not my words. This is straight from the Book of Revelation, from the words of John, a man who walked with Jesus, who knew Jesus, who Jesus touched. According to the Bible, God's anger is very apparent. This is the coming judgment foretold.

Intrinsically we are aware of what displeases God. Is it a mystery as to what you or I might do if we were appointed to judge the evil of this world? How could the oppression of innocent women and children, or the mutilation and murder of human life not stir up a righteous indignation in any one of us? Who wouldn't want to destroy evil in the most powerful and ferocious way? Deep down I can only begin to empathize with God and realize His anger against the evil of this world is justified. In fact, many of us are probably grateful for the intense ferocity and rage God will unleash against the present evil many of us so vehemently hate! Who can argue with the extreme fierceness God has for injustice and cruelty.

Before the wrath of God begins we have the opportunity to make peace with God. Only God knows how much time remains. The Book of Proverbs says, "The fear of the LORD is the beginning of wisdom…" (Proverbs 9:10). Perhaps the fear of God is intended to help steer us toward our need for salvation. We seem to have something in us motivated by worry, but is worry what the fear of God is really about? What is fear and how am I supposed to fear God?

The Fear of God

Perhaps the common ground of fear will help unite us. I do see dramatic moves toward unity among people in the midst of calamity. When it comes to my personal life, I hope that I'm wise enough to act responsibly before life turns into a crisis, producing a "fear" in me that ultimately forces me to resolve that which got me into a predicament. I hope to prevent my life getting out of hand in this way. Maybe as long as I'm stubborn I'll be dealing with my crises, but maybe understanding fear will help me to avoid them. When I stop to think about fear I think of being frightened or scared. But the "fear of the LORD" found in the Bible is different. It's a respectful fear, awe in reverence for God. Proverbs says, "…fear of the LORD prolongs life, But the years of the wicked will be shortened" (Proverbs 10:27). "The fear of the LORD is to hate evil; Pride and arrogance and the evil way…" (Proverbs 8:13).

The Book of Proverbs continues on: "In the fear of the LORD there is strong confidence, And His children will have refuge. The fear of the LORD is a fountain of life, That one may avoid the snares of death" (Proverbs 14:26-27). "The fear of the LORD is the instruction for wisdom…" (Proverbs 15:33), "…And by the fear of the LORD one keeps away from evil" (Proverbs 16:6). "The reward of humility *and* the fear of the Lord Are riches, honor and life" (Proverbs 22:4).

This kind of fear brings me closer to God. It's a good fear. When I think back to when I've sat on the edge of a cliff and looked down and out at Yosemite's valley, I feel the great beauty and magnitude of God's created wonder. The precarious nature of where I sat is clear. "Nature" is more powerful than I realize—just like me not thinking to bring enough water on my hike. Potentially, it's very possible to die if I'm not careful enough. A *healthy* sense of fear for the place I sat helped protect me. I don't want to ever fall off. Out of care and concern I have respect for the beauty and danger I beheld sitting upon that edge.

Maybe this is how to fear God—honor and respect for God's great beauty and glory. Jesus said, "Do not fear those who kill the body but are unable to kill the soul; but rather fear Him who is able to destroy both soul and body in hell" (Matthew 10:28). It's a fact that the power of life and death are in the hand of God. If fearing God means respecting God for His mighty position, then truly I fear God. I want to be drawn into God's protection, away from death and destruction.

My fear of God amounts to knowing God's might and power, and how the universe can be created or destroyed at His will. I don't feel terrorized by this. God loves and protects me. On God's side I am secure. Not because I'm afraid of God, but because life is with God. I enjoy being part of God's plan. I enjoy working with God. In life I recognize there are things that help me and things that hurt me. Dishonor and disrespect for others; stealing, violating innocence life, deceiving others for personal gain, contracting a disease from premarital sex, or committing adultery, or worse, spreading disease to the person I married—these things will devastate my life and others. These are the things that hurt others and me. I should fear these sinful acts because of what God says they are devised to do.

A healthy fear of God should serve to help make positive choices, in big and small ways, for others and myself. I want to stop creating problems. I feel that I'm already starting to possess a fear that encourages me to resolve matters through forgiveness, and to compensate for the wrong I do. The fear of God is about acting responsibly. I see my fear of God better directing my conscience to do the right things. Perhaps Godly fear will keep a cold and hardened heart from ever forming.

I do tremble at the thought of total separation from God. It would be "hell." I don't want to experience eternal suffering. The fear of God motivates me to know God, to understand who God is, and why God desires certain things for my life. Out of love and protection, God just wants me to make the right choices—blessings, not curses.

When I look at the wrathful face upon Half Dome, I do not fear what God will do to me. The blood of Christ now protects me, and the wrath of God that is scheduled will pass over me. I am comforted to know God will deal with evil. Though mercy has come in the person of Jesus, the wrathful face of God ultimately represents divine justice.

Justice and Mercy

Since the day God revealed the sign on Half Dome to me I haven't really been discussing it openly with many other people because I'm still working to make sense of it. I feel as if I've just bitten off a huge chunk of reality and I'm chewing, and chewing, and chewing. Understanding the implications of what God has put onto the face of Half Dome is a major growth process happening internally. It seems I'm laboring diligently just to swallow all the truth being presented. I want to talk about it with everyone, I really do, but I'm just not ready to. Fortunately my step-mom Jenny has been an open ear for much of this eye-opening experience. Her family had invited me to come to Yosemite when I first laid eyes on Half Dome.

Jenny is a Christian and so I directed many of my questions about God her way. She gave me answers as she understood things to be, but most times she directed me to search the Bible. My struggle to make reason of the sign and understand the words of the Bible moves me to challenge her about whatever isn't making sense. Thank goodness she is a woman of great patience because she really helps manage all my skepticism. One issue I've been challenging her on is the issue of why God lets evil exist.

When I look broadly out into the world's scene, unnecessary catastrophe and suffering is evident. Apart from God and even the devil, I have to admit I see humans as being the architects behind a great deal of plight and suffering. In part, realizing this gives me hope. It tells me that for the most part, humankind sows the seeds of every situation—reaping bad things and reaping good things. Still I don't understand why evil exists if God is in control. So I ask Jenny if God is capable of doing or allowing anything and everything in life, what's the deal with evil? How could a loving God let bad things happen? Masses of people throughout the world are starving at this very moment. The long-term effect of pollution could potentially kill us if we aren't careful. Governments and nations oppress and murder their own people. "Why does God seem to let destruction and evil have its way with us?" I ask.

Jenny tells me to trust God for what I do not understand, but this is not the answer I'm looking for. She persists to impress upon me that God is "just" and in control, and that everything will work out according to His plan. So then maybe the answer is in understanding the justice of God, but how does the justice of God work in natural disasters and catastrophic suffering, death and destruction? Is it because we deserve it? Many times I think, "How can a loving God do such things or let them happen?" I also hear a lot of people blaming the devil for challenges and suffering we face, but I once heard someone say, "The devil gets a lot of bad press." I believe the point made was that the devil is sometimes nowhere to be found in our difficult situations, and that we tend to blame the devil for our own consequences that God is simply allowing.

Other words for justice are: fairness, impartiality, righteousness, evenhandedness, honesty, and integrity. When I engage the Bible to study the justice of God, I'm taken to various scriptures and begin to see that justice starts with integrity.

"God is not a man, that He should lie,

Nor a son of man, that He should repent;

Has He said, and will He not do it? Or has He spoken,

and will He not make it good?" (Numbers 23:19)

"For I, the LORD, do not change…" (Malachi 3:6)

"Every good thing given and every perfect gift

is from above, coming down from the Father of lights, with whom there

is no variation or shifting shadow

[or *shadow of turning*]" (James 1:17)

"…the hope of eternal life, which God, who cannot lie, promised long

ages ago" (Titus 1:2)

"…it is impossible for God to lie…" (Hebrews 6:18).

These scriptures communicate the integrity of God's words and that God is unchanging. They say that God does not lie. Perhaps God's nature is bound to an eternal integrity that is simply, yet unyieldingly fixed to judge rightly. The justice of God would therefore be obligated to follow through with the laws of physics, of spirit, and whatever God has made or promised. The justice of God appears to be already set in motion. God is set to deliver consequences according to actions. Our evil actions will unfortunately reap His wrath, but what about the mercy of God?

A passage of old recounts the choices of a nation: "At one moment I might speak concerning a nation or concerning a kingdom to uproot, to pull down, or to destroy *it;* if that nation against which I have spoken turns from its evil, I will relent concerning the calamity I planned to bring on it. Or at another moment I might speak concerning a nation or concerning a kingdom to build up or to plant *it;* if it does evil in My sight by not obeying My voice, then I will think better of the good with which I had promised to bless it" (Jeremiah 18:7-10).

It seems that God allows an opening for His judgment to be diverted when people choose to turn away from evil ways. Would this then be God changing His mind? Does this mean you or I or anyone is able to change the mind of God? It is written that Jesus is "...the Alpha and the Omega, the first and the last, the beginning and the end," (Revelation 22:13). If this indicates God sees all things, God would therefore know if and when we will turn to Him—away from our sin, away from evil ways, and ultimately, away from destruction.

This would maintain that God's mind does not change; God purely acts according to His foreknowledge of our true heart. It's God's choice and in His nature to have kindness toward the repentant heart: "When God saw their deeds, that they turned from their wicked way, then God relented concerning the calamity which He had declared He would bring upon them. And He did not do it" (Jonah 3:10). It's not hard for me to trust that God "saw their deeds" before the foundations of the earth because it's written that Jesus knows the beginning to the end. "Nevertheless He looked upon their distress When He heard their cry; And He remembered His covenant for their sake, And relented according to the greatness of His lovingkindness" (Psalm 106:44-45). God reveals mercy by not delivering His judgment upon hearing our cry for mercy.

Perhaps the sheer existence of our "free will" represents the mercy and justice of God all at once. I'm not a robot yet there remains the redemption for my wrongdoing. "Perhaps [we] will listen and everyone will turn from his evil way, that [God] may repent of the calamity which [God is] planning to do to them because of the evil of their deeds" (Jeremiah 26:3). I don't think God desires to bring destruction. The Bible speaks to the gentleness of God: "...For He is gracious and compassionate, Slow to anger, abounding in lovingkindness And relenting of evil. Who knows whether He will not turn and relent And leave a blessing behind Him...." (Joel 2:13-14).

God's mercy is shown to accompany His wrath and judgment. This to me reveals the love of God. I find the following set of verses that were written by the Apostle Paul to explain our circumstance in profound detail, rationalizing the justice of God and revealing His mercy. The Apostle John sums up the reason Jesus came for us and how the justice of God applies to our situation. The final verse concludes how God wants people to respond in kind. These thirty-two verses capture the human condition and show the sense of balance between justice and mercy as they pertain to the universal judgment of God:

"…The kindness of God leads you to repentance? But because of your stubbornness and unrepentant heart you are storing up wrath for yourself in the day of wrath and revelation of the righteous judgment of God, who WILL RENDER TO EACH PERSON ACCORDING TO HIS DEEDS: to those who by perseverance in doing good seek for glory and honor and immortality, eternal life; but to those who are selfishly ambitious and do not obey the truth, but obey unrighteousness, wrath and indignation. *There will be* tribulation and distress for every soul of man who does evil, of the Jew first and also of the Greek, but glory and honor and peace to everyone who does good, to the Jew first and also to the Greek. For there is no partiality with God. For all who have sinned without the Law will also perish without the Law, and all who have sinned under the Law will be judged by the Law; for *it is* not the hearers of the Law *who* are just before God, but the doers of the Law will be justified. For when Gentiles who do not have the Law do instinctively the things of the Law, these, not having the Law, are a law to themselves, in that they show the work of the Law written in their hearts, their conscience bearing witness and their thoughts alternately accusing or else defending them, on the day when, according to my gospel, God will judge the secrets of men through Christ Jesus" (Romans 2:4-16).

"Now we know that whatever the Law says, it speaks to those who are under the Law, so that every mouth may be closed and all the world may become accountable to God; because by the works of the Law no flesh will be justified in His sight; for through the Law *comes* the knowledge of sin. But now apart from the Law *the* righteousness of God has been manifested, being witnessed by the Law and the Prophets, even *the* righteousness of God through faith in Jesus Christ for all those who believe; for there is no distinction; for all have sinned and fall short of the glory of God, being justified as a gift by His grace through the redemption which is in Christ Jesus; whom God displayed publicly as a propitiation in His blood through faith. *This was* to demonstrate His righteousness, because in the forbearance of God He passed over the sins previously committed; for the demonstration,

I say, of His righteousness at the present time, so that He would be just and the justifier of the one who has faith in Jesus" (Romans 3:19-26).

"Therefore, having been justified by faith, we have peace with God through our Lord Jesus Christ, through whom also we have obtained our introduction by faith into this grace in which we stand; and we exult in hope of the glory of God. And not only this, but we also exult in our tribulations, knowing that tribulation brings about perseverance; and perseverance, proven character; and proven character, hope; and hope does not disappoint, because the love of God has been poured out within our hearts through the Holy Spirit who was given to us" (Romans 5:1-5).

"For God so loved the world, that He gave His only begotten Son, that whoever believes in Him shall not perish, but have eternal life. For God did not send the Son into the world to judge the world, but that the world might be saved through Him. He who believes in Him is not judged; he who does not believe has been judged already, because he has not believed in the name of the only begotten Son of God. This is the judgment, that the Light has come into the world, and men loved the darkness rather than the Light, for their deeds were evil. For everyone who does evil hates the Light, and does not come to the Light for fear that his deeds will be exposed. But he who practices the truth comes to the Light, so that his deeds may be manifested as having been wrought in God" (John 3:16-21). "…if you confess with your mouth Jesus *as* Lord, and believe in your heart that God raised Him from the dead, you will be saved…" (Romans 10:9).

These thirty-two verses contain mass amounts of information. My Bible gives what seems an endless host of references that take me all over the Bible. This block of scripture is something to be read over and over to help map the words charted. I see my sin as the target of God's wrath more than my soul as the target. The kindness of God has put forth the remedy through Jesus as redemption for the transgression of Adam handed down to me. He wants my soul, but He doesn't want me to hold onto my sin. I have to admit there is a part of me that thinks this human situation in which I find myself is ridiculous and God couldn't really be looking at things this way—could He? At the same time I don't want to be stubborn and reason as though the sin of Adam is not my fault. If I'm really being honest about the life I've been living and the choices I've made, I have to admit I've done wrong. Some of my decisions do amount to sin. I can't escape the reality that the justice of God demands God judge all things fairly, which means by the standards of God I am guilty of the same transgression of Adam—this is justice.

The standard of God, His "Law," is like an "eternal filter" that captures sin. In turn I am held back from eternity because sin is attached to me. Apparently God's holiness does not allow the crime of disobedience to contaminate heaven or His presence, but it's also apparent that Jesus came to solve my problem of separation. At this point the number one thing God wants me to realize is that there is *nothing* I can do to inherit eternal life, *except* trust Jesus for doing what I could not do. Christ offers the free gift of salvation in light of my corrupted condition—this is mercy. In response, I choose to follow Jesus for the assurance of eternal life.

This is part of what Jenny means by trusting in God for everything to work according to His plan. Jesus is the plan. I don't know that we'll ever be able to fully answer all the questions we have about natural disasters and suffering and oppression, but maybe it's already clear. Maybe it's as simple as being our fault because we choose to sin. We have chosen to put ourselves in the path of turmoil and God's wrath because we sin. In the same way, we choose to place ourselves in situations that may turn out disastrous. If a ferocious storm is bearing down, the best solution is to reach a safe place if we want to assure survival. I know I'm greatly simplifying here, but I see the parallel: the great storm of God is on the radar screen, and our trust in Christ is the safe place that assures our survival.

Our common-ground foundation is the sin of humankind, the wrath of God, the justice of God, and now, the mercy of God in Christ. We share these things in common. We also share hopes and goals. We want to end extreme suffering, poverty, and oppression. We want to provide education for all children and people. We want equal rights. We want to cure deadly disease. We want to preserve the environment for future generations. We want unity among all people, cultures, and nations. We want to leave our world in a better place than we were born into. We also know these dreams can only become real when we work together to fulfill them. Reaching common ground is not an option. It is a necessity.

Chapter Six

The True Realm

"I can see how it might be possible
for a man to look down upon the earth and be an atheist,
but I cannot conceive how he could look up into the heavens
and say there is no God."
– Abraham Lincoln

Heaven is my ultimate home, yet earth is where I live. This future paradise I'm destined for has me craving to know more about it. Where is the kingdom of heaven? What is the kingdom of heaven? I think for me to fully grasp the relationship between heaven and earth I need to make better sense of religion. This will lead me to work through some issues I have with faith. Maybe I'm troubled with religion because I don't understand it, but maybe there are just general problems. When it comes to faith, I get frustrated with the paradox of it. Most of this is because I tend to be very logical and analytical, and I think faith is being abused in some ways. By examining religion and faith I hope to be able to see the kingdom of God and the heart of it all, recognize my destiny.

I'm not going to church yet. I say *yet* because part of me thinks I should. The other part of me is afraid or not ready. I tell myself that one day I will, but for now I'm preparing myself by learning all that I can on my own. Don't get me wrong, I've been to church before, but I haven't committed myself to a specific church community. I guess I'm trying to avoid being "duped." I also don't want to live through someone else telling me what the Bible says until I know the Bible myself. That's one of the main reasons I've been including so much Bible scripture in this book. I want to know as much first hand as I possibly can. I assume you do too. I think it's best if we actually read what the Bible is saying about a particular topic. What a concept!

My Grandpa Bill is a Christian, and he is very dedicated to going to church.

I don't know him that well, but the times my brother and I have spent with him while we were growing up, felt positive. Grandpa Bill is Jenny's father, whom she loves and respects tremendously. I went to see him in 1994 to discuss some of my questions and issues with religion. About two years have passed since that first day I stepped onto the valley floor to see Half Dome. Bill was also there during that trip, but I didn't make it known to him what was going on. At this point in time though, I feel ready to talk a little bit about it with him. He was happy to have me come by.

I started off by showing him a photograph of Half Dome and pointing out the images I see. I explained that as a result of witnessing this and studying the Bible I have given my life to Christ. My excitement and zeal are very apparent to him through my passionate outlook on life I am expressing. I went on to ask him what I should do about this sign on Half Dome. "You need to get to know Jesus like the back of your hand," said Grandpa Bill, "You also need to find a good church." Oh, there it was! I liked the getting to know Jesus part because I was already doing that, but the going to church part was not what I wanted to hear. He said, "It's great to see your zeal, but I'd like to see how you feel about all this in ten years."

My words don't begin to do him justice. When I read them back I might be making him out to sound cold and callous, but that couldn't be further from the truth. This just happens to be what stuck to me the most. Grandpa Bill said that when going to church, "Many coals burn hot together," and the ones that are off to the side, tend to burn out hastily. I took his words to heart. He was happy to now see me walking with the Lord, because I know he had prayed for me as I was growing up. I think he might have even been there that day when I was eight when my brother and I prayed to ask Jesus into our heart in the swimming pool. I feel that I am now more obligated to grapple with what religion is because Grandpa Bill has challenged me to go to church.

Making Sense of Religion

So what's the real deal with religion? Maybe I fought off the Lord in the past because of my reservations about big, established religion. It's definitely keeping some of us from committing to Christ, right? I was amazed when I discovered what the Bible actually states about religion. James wrote: "Pure and undefiled religion in the sight of *our* God and Father is this: to visit orphans and widows in their distress, *and* to keep oneself unstained by the world" (James 1:27). This is so simple, and after reading this it's easy to see that human beings have greatly complicated the true meaning of religion. Apart from people building "shrines of ego and prestige" and "thrones of power," we still can't say that everything about church is bad. In fact, as I look deeper into what's being done around the world in the name of God's "church" I see more positive actions than negative ones.

Unfortunately my idea of religion has been tainted and damaged by the weight and weirdness the church sometimes burdens people with, to say the least. Headlines in the media about immorality and deception within the church have cast a negative shadow on religion in general—at least for me it has. When we add in all the violence and division spread across history, it is no wonder people are scratching their heads and asking, "Why would I want to be a part of that?" In spite of this, I have to be fair and ask, "Is it possible I'm throwing out the greater good with the lesser bad?"

It's a beautiful thing that great deeds are done and arts of worship raised in honor of God. Great ministries like that of Mother Teresa and countless others, noble works such as The Sistine Chapel, the Basilica of Saint Peter, and inspiring art from the age of the Renaissance are some of the most powerful expressions, to name just a few. Yet even with this, I see the possibility of losing sight of God when the *institution* and the *works* themselves become the focus of our adoration instead of God. Maybe this is part of the reason contributing to the lack of peace and unity within religion, at least with Christianity. I find it hard to believe this is really the way things have to be amidst so much good being done.

In the spirit of "true religion" I find Jesus directing us to help care for those in need: "For I was hungry, and you gave Me *something* to eat; I was thirsty, and you gave Me *something* to drink; I was a stranger, and you invited Me in; naked, and you clothed Me; I was sick, and you visited Me; I was in prison, and you came to Me" (Matthew 25:35-36). Jesus also said, "The kingdom of heaven is like leaven, which a woman took and hid in three pecks of flour until it was all leavened" (Matthew 13:33). My Bible study notes indicate that this verse symbolizes growth, and the inner working of the Holy Spirit. It's easily argued that Christianity has perhaps grown to be the most benevolent influence in all of history. Considering these verses and benevolent circumstances, true religion reveals itself as being more about helping people than anything else. If the priority of religion is not James 1:27 and Matthew 25:35-36, it's fair for me to conclude that religion therefore misses the point. Jesus gave His disciples yet another commandment when He said, "A new commandment I give to you, that you love one another, even as I have loved you, that you also love one another. By this all men will know that you are My disciples, if you have love for one another" (John 13:32-33). We're all called to love and help others at some level. Does this then mean we're all called to be a part of religion?

When I look back through history I see that religion tends to gravitate toward the quest for power while carrying out true Godly service—even in some ways religion still does this today. Like a government or authoritative entity, the church becomes attracted to power. Once the church is drawn into its natural position of authority, the quest to satiate its appetite drives the mode of self-preservation to protect its power. This unfortunately becomes the priority over the original purpose of empowering its people to perform the true works of religion as James and Jesus spell out. I think this is one place where religion tends to go bad. Satan is presented with an opportunity to take advantage of the church by using the thirst for power as a tool to turn people away from God. At least this is what I'm assessing. When established religion or a particular church is caught up in controversy, I struggle to see how I'm supposed to have an intimate relationship with God in all of this.

It's unmistakable that just about all segments of the church at one time or another have a history of controlling its congregation with false justifications of authority. This is exactly what I'm afraid of. I don't want my faith in God to be exploited through fear and manipulation. This could only serve as an obstacle between God and me. I'm uneasy that my journey with God will somehow get sidetracked if I start down the religious or church path. Part of me dislikes what I'm saying because I don't want to be bashing the church. After all, the church is all over the New Testament and I've read verses that tell me God prizes the church. I know the whole church isn't corrupt, just parts of it. Still, I have reason to be concerned about the leaders of modern day "religion" and religious establishments.

Obviously enough of us are apprehensive for a reason. The fact that multitudes of people who want a relationship with God are very skeptical of church says a lot. It couldn't just be our sin wanting to keep us out of church, but I also realize sin is partly the case. Either way, it cannot be good.

I found that Jesus validated some of my concern when He said: "…woe to you…because you shut off the kingdom of heaven from people; for you do not enter in yourselves, nor do you allow those who are entering to go in…woe to you…because you travel around on sea and land to make one proselyte; and when he becomes one, you make him twice as much a son of hell as yourselves…So you, too, outwardly appear righteous to men, but inwardly you are full of hypocrisy and lawlessness…You serpents, you brood of vipers, how will escape the sentence of hell?" (Matthew 23:13, 15, 28, 33). He was referring to the religious leaders of His day here. These are harsh words, but I can see this happening even today. Parts of the whole Christian church presume its "positional" authority as "spiritual" authority, putting people in spiritual bondage and distracting the church body itself from the true religion of helping others. These are actually cult-like tendencies leading to egocentric organizations that rob God's people of the very freedom spiritual leaders are obligated to instill.

In the midst of all my frustration about church, I'm comforted to see true religion from the perspective of Jesus. Perhaps I don't have to fear being a part of the church, because whichever church I attend deviates from the true religion of God I am commanded by the very Bible to stay out of spiritual oppression. The Apostle Paul has helped me put on the full armor of God. He doesn't want to see me pulled away from Jesus because I'm being controlled or abused by others. The Bible hasn't made it clear to me that the church is somehow allowed to raise itself above the purposes of God. The Bible does make clear that we're charged to pull down strongholds that exalt themselves above the knowledge of God. I don't see myself attacking the church, just helping to hold it accountable. Since I'm a Christian now, it's my church too.

This means I can be a part of the solution rather than enabling religion's problems. If I allow people to control me, I in turn feed the power of those who seek to control. Everyone has the opportunity to help God's church when it is suffering. Fortunately I do see parts of the church thriving according to God's intention. I'm not going to allow misguided religion to hold me back from fulfilling my destiny in God. Along the way we can help make His church all He intends it to be. Religion is ultimately what we make of it.

One of my biggest stumbling blocks about the church has been the sexual abuse and violation of little children by religious leaders. This has got to be one of the worst offenses of all. It's so terrible that not only does it physically and emotionally scar a person for life; the violation causes us to turn away from God. The religious leader we trusted has performed evil. We say, "How can this be of God?" because we know it's not. We then reject the institution responsible for housing these evil acts.

Jesus said, "…whoever causes one of these little ones who believe in Me to stumble, it would be better for him to have a heavy millstone hung around his neck, and to be drowned in the depth of the sea" (Matthew 18:6). Jesus weighs in here. I don't take this as He's commanding we drown people either. I gather He's saying the violation of turning people away from God is a bad, bad thing. It's evil to exploit the innocence of children and turn harmless hearts away from God. It's even worse when a place of refuge turns out to be an ambush of Satan. Immediate accountability needs to be enforced, and these leaders who are sexually abusing children should be banned from leading. Let God judge the soul, but let people move to correct the problem.

I am compelled to express my feelings about this. My heart is torn just realizing the agony a person's spirit must go through after being sexually abused, to then struggle by wondering if God did this to them. This all arises because of *someone else* who actuality stole their trust. It's just plain evil. I fear the judgment of God on the church for this one issue alone. Sexual abuse and the preservation of evil leadership within the body of Christ must be stopped immediately! This should stir up a righteous indignation within us to change the circumstances, because if we wait for God to act we will undoubtedly wish *we* would have. By continuing to allow this to go on we're letting Satan lead parts of God's church.

I get so mad realizing what's going on, but I've got to stop myself from ranting! It's no mystery why we're turned off from church and religion in a big way. "God help us heal from this type of sin and violation! Heal those who've been violated! Convict the heart of your people to force resolution here! Help me to see what you want me to see about religion and Your church!" Compose me Lord so I can actually do something about it.

It's very evident that sin has the capability of pulling us away from the goodness of God, leaving us wrestling for freedom from hellish abuse. Add Satan's strategy to this mix and we've got a whole lot of challenges facing us. And no matter what our worldview and what our life professes, we've got to work extra hard not contradict ourselves for the sake of God and unity. The Apostle Paul said to, "…examine everything *carefully*; and hold fast to that which is good; abstain from every form [or appearance] of evil" (1 Thessalonians 5:21-22). The last thing I think anyone wants to let happen is to have all our efforts torn down because we let our sin or the appearance of evil turn each other away from God. The will of Satan would be accomplished.

Faith

Faith is another hurdle I'm working to get over, though not nearly as big an obstacle as established religion has been. It's evident that the power of faith is very strong, and that I do in fact exercise it. It's very hard indeed to argue that faith doesn't have the power to change a person's life. It does. At the same time, while supplying unfathomable hope and encouragement it may also be fueling great division. I'm asking myself, "Could the strife and rage of the world, genuinely emanating from personal lives, be a result of misguided faith?" The inner convictions born through faith position our hearts to take certain stands, but could we be abusing faith by taking advantage of it in certain ways?

I am intensely intrigued with faith. I'm someone who searches for facts and searches to place trust in what is known. I don't want to rely upon spiritual sensation alone, because self-deception is a reality. So when it comes to my own well being I think it's unwise to take leaps of devotion into non-significance, based on a "feeling" or even a strong conviction. But the Bible speaks of faith. So I am bound to figure out what the Bible means by it. The most simple and direct description states: "…faith is the assurance of *things* hoped for, the conviction of things not seen" (Hebrews 11:1). The Bible records many examples of faith—faith in being healed, faith in providing or being provided for, faith in how we should live, faith in God, and faith, of course, in Christ.

In the book of Hebrews, chapter eleven, verses one through forty tell about the acts of people who were prompted by God to do something for God. They weren't given the facts and details about how to accomplish what they were about to attempt, but they had faith God would lead them to succeed—faith to escape eminent peril; faith of inheritance; faith to bear children; faith about how to help others. Day to day, they had faith that God would guide them and see them through the convictions He had placed on their hearts. This section of scripture, nonetheless, tells of their faith to pursue the God-given burdens of their hearts. They obviously had an intimate relationship with God and most would say that they had "faith" in God, "believing with their heart." This much is true. But how much do we factor in their tangible encounters with the Almighty? Perhaps their tangible encounters with God did not require "faith," but simply the mental capacity to comprehend their actual physical encounter they previously had with God.

The first recorded encounter Moses had with God was intense and physical. Moses wrote: "The angel of the Lord appeared to him in a blazing fire from the midst of a bush; and he looked, and behold, the bush was burning with fire, yet the bush was not consumed. So Moses said, 'I must turn aside now and see this marvelous sight, why the bush is not burned up.' When the Lord saw that he turned aside to look, God called to him from the midst of the bush and said, 'Moses, Moses!' And he said, 'Here I am.' Then He said, 'Do not come near here; remove your sandals from your feet, for the place on which you are standing is holy ground.' He said also, 'I am the God of your father, the God of Abraham, the God of Isaac, and the God of Jacob.' Then Moses hid his face, for he was afraid to look at God" (Exodus 3:2-6).

Moses "saw" and "heard" and "spoke." This account details a physical event between God and Moses. At this point, was Moses having faith that God was real? According to this, Moses simply *knew* God was real. When you read on from Exodus 3:6, you will read the story about how Moses was then required to have *faith to do* a seemingly impossible task God asked him to do. This is what the eleventh chapter of Hebrews is about—having faith in the plan God is asking us to accomplish.

I think of a friend I know. I think of my family. Do I have "faith" they exist or that they are real? No. I don't hope they're real, I know they are. I physically see and experience their presence. The "faith" I have in them doesn't pertain to whether or not they physically exist—it's all about my trust in them for what they will *say* or *do* in light of our relationship. It's the same with God. God can be known when we seek the truth, but it requires faith to do what God leads us to do—through our spirit, confirmed through the physical and situational reality, and through what is written in the Bible. The Holy Spirit becomes my guide Who will then lead me through the correct steps to fulfill what God is asking of me.

Consider the twelve disciples of Jesus along with others who physically knew Him and spent time with Him on earth. After Jesus had been crucified, did they have "faith" or "know" that He had risen from the dead? Jesus spoke in regards to this. "Then He said to Thomas, 'Reach here with your finger, and see My hands; reach here your hand and put it into My side; and do not be unbelieving, but believing.' Thomas answered and said to Him, 'My Lord and my God!' Jesus said to him, 'Because you have seen Me, have you believed? Blessed *are* they who did not see, and *yet* believed" (John 20:27-29). So the answer is "both"—Thomas *knew* Jesus had risen because he was able to now touch Him, and others had faith *before* they saw Him. Jesus having praised them for their faith in His resurrection even before they were physically able to confirm Him being alive reveals the perplexing nature of faith. I suppose the empty tomb was technically the first piece of evidence of His resurrection, and apparently that was all some needed in order to trust Jesus was alive—but they still believed without physically seeing Jesus. I conclude that the reason Jesus said they were blessed is because they were in fact trusting God, and Thomas wasn't.

Even with this, let's not stop and assume that God *never* intended to physically reveal Himself as being resurrected to them at some point either. Let's face it, not much time had passed in between the empty tomb and the room they were gathered in where Jesus appeared in His resurrected body. Perhaps God was providing the opportunity to help them recognize that their faith was indeed being placed in something "real." Interestingly enough Jesus did not say, "Who *do* not see Me." He said, "Who *did* not see." "*Did*" means done. "*Do*" means to resolve. Now the last thing I want to do here is start a game of semantics. My point is that God expects us to base our faith on evidence. No one, not one of the twelve had faith Jesus was resurrected until after the tomb was empty. They were either "mourning and weeping" or "refused to believe it" (Mark 16:10-11). I encourage you to read the whole account for yourself. You will see that even Jesus' closest disciples ran to the tomb to confirm that it was empty for a fact. I conclude that even the ones who eventually believed without seeing had the fact of the empty tomb to base their faith upon. I therefore reason that the resurrection of Jesus, which created the empty tomb, was the final piece of evidence required to complete one's faith in Christ for salvation. The equation might look like this:

Old Testament prophetic indications about Christ

+

The full earthly ministry of Jesus and His crucifixion

+

The Resurrection and the empty tomb

=

The essential evidence
God expected the disciples to trust at that very point in time

I'm venturing to state that John 20:29 is God's way of saying that all is needed for us to believe is everything He's already given to us. Jesus confirmed this when He said, "This generation is a wicked generation; it seeks for a sign, and yet no sign will be given to it but the sign of Jonah. For just as Jonah became a sign to the Ninevites, so will the Son of Man be to this generation" (Luke 11:29-30). In light of this, I don't see where God ever expects our faith to be blind (not based on evidence)—maybe bold, but certainly not blind. God has provided the sign of Christ. I suppose God could have stopped here with this sign, but what about Thomas or me and maybe you? Obviously God provides even more signs. First we poke at the truth, then maybe we grab for it, and hopefully like Thomas we give in to the evidence. Fortunately for us, Jesus reveals Himself despite skepticism. God's mercy goes to great lengths to help us see Him. I don't think God tries to hide either. It's simple—many of us just doubt or don't put forth the effort to examine the evidence already existing. Instead we put forth the energy to make faith into something obscure. Whether we intend to or not, we end up usurping faith when we license the use of "blind faith" so we can posture our hearts to believe whatever we imagine as being true. This is how I see faith being abused. This intrusion upon faith creates confusion and apathy throughout the world, ultimately producing conflict. We might say the confusion is over "conflicting" truths, but there's no such thing. Satan has just managed to deceive us yet again.

This is why I've been struggling with faith, because it's been made out to be something God didn't design. Now, I'm really starting to grasp what it truly is. To me faith simply equals trust. Whether it is better or worse to want physical proof is not the point—God gives it. It is, however, vital we seek God for the evidence of His existence so that our trust can be placed in what is real. Jesus said, "So I say to you, ask, and it will be given to you; seek, and you will find; knock, and it will be opened to you" (Luke 11:9). I literally have no excuse for not obtaining the truth about God. The moment we will physically meet God, whether to be condemned or rewarded, is the moment our faith will be tested conclusively. *Knowing* things for certain where evidence abounds serves to fortify and transform our faith from being belief to becoming knowledge. This is the fusion of truth and perception. This is the intended destination I set out for—to *know* the reality of God. I yearned for knowledge about God, yet did not stop learning about all the ways in which God is evident. As a result I'm able to place my trust in what is known. This to me is worshipping God with my mind as well as my heart, soul, and strength.

Building on Solid Ground

Today in the second millennium since Jesus walked this earth, God is mercifully revealing Himself in a very radical way through Half Dome. It continues to be the case that a mountain of evidence can be known about God. Truth reveals God, and God reveals truth. My convictions are based upon knowledge of the truth. Again, I turn to the Bible where Jesus tells a story:

"Therefore everyone who hears these words of Mine and acts on them, may be compared to a wise man who built his house on the rock. And the rain fell, and the floods came, and the winds blew and slammed against that house; and *yet* it did not fall, for it had been founded on the rock. Everyone who hears these words of Mine and does not act on them, will be like a foolish man who built his house on the sand. The rain fell, and the floods came, and the winds blew and slammed against that house; and it fell—and great was its fall" (Matthew 7:24-27).

God calls us to build on solid ground. Truth is the solid ground; sand is deception. The sands of pure pleasure are not worthy ground to build upon. Delightful as they may seem, the day of great trial is set to wash the sands away and everything built upon them—maybe even beforehand. There is no excuse to lack understanding about my foundation. It's realistic to know the foundation I live upon. Sand was my foundation, but I moved onto the solid foundation of truth. Now Jesus assures the preservation of my life before the great storm approaches.

We've heard it said, it's been written into movie scripts, acted out in front of the cameras: "It only matters what you believe." This would be correct only if it didn't matter what's true in the first place. However, since truth can be known it unquestionably matters that I place my trust in the solid foundation of truth. Since God is real and has established Jesus as Savior, I place my trust in Christ.

"God, Continue to show me the solid foundation on which to build. Give us the faith to do great things—small and mighty." Jesus said, "...for truly I say to you, if you have the faith the size of a mustard seed, you will say to this mountain, 'Move from here to there,' and it will move; and nothing will be impossible to you" (Matthew 17:20). God help me to have faith in the purposes and plans You have set before me, and to identify the solid ground.

Of everything in me, sincerity has been key to helping me see God. The prophet Jeremiah spoke for God saying, "You will seek Me and find *Me* when you search for Me with all your heart" (Jeremiah 29:13). I think God is first seen with the heart and soul. Then the more we seek God the more evidence is revealed. "Blessed are the pure in heart, for they shall see God" (Matthew 5:8). There could be a book written alone about what "pure of heart" means, but I think honesty and sincerity are a good start to having a pure heart on this side of eternity.

My faith in God began with a genuine desire to know the truth—whatever the truth ended up being. Why should it matter what the truth is? What matters most, is that it gets found. And upon finding, it's clear the truth exists to understand. And upon understanding, I'm given the choice to accept or deny it. If I don't like what I find, the only other option is to change God. I'm sure Satan would like me to think this way and have us believe that we can somehow change the image of God or get around Jesus.

My faith in God does not make God real. God is God no matter what we believe. It's not a matter of questioning whether or not anyone's faith is genuine. It better be. The question is, "How mature is our faith?" How deep have we examined it? If faith in God is ever to be properly exercised it must be placed in the reality of who God is and what God is really commanding of us—only what God is commanding of us: nothing more and nothing less. Either our faith is misled because it's placed in the devices, notions, and religions of man that control us, or we have faith in the truth about God and realize we are only bound by God's principles and the limitations we impose on ourselves.

Satan would prefer to have us entangled in our own affairs, overlooking the true reality of God, thinking, believing, and having faith that we are doing what God wants, but fooled about knowing who God really is. Sincerity leads me *to* the right direction. Constant examination of my path keeps me *in* the right direction. Boldness helps me stay the course, and humility safeguards my journey along the way. If I believe I have life one hundred percent figured out, arrogance will pull me into the psychosis of my own agenda. I become unwilling to listen to another person's perception of reality that God might actually be guiding me to see with.

Putting our feelings and faith aside for just a moment, Jesus being God and Savior is supported by more facts than anything else in the history of the world. No one person or entity, past or present, ever claiming to be God and Savior has had this much evidence on their side making the case. Jesus leads the way with the most corroboration. I simply side with reality. I place my trust in this concrete knowledge. The facts exist for anyone to examine. Now with the image revealed on Half Dome, it is evermore convincing that Jesus is who He says He is. So I propose a solution to our dilemma of faith: instead of having faith in faith let's have faith to trust in truth.

Putting forth the utmost effort to place faith in what is real will help our world to see eye-to-eye and actually establish vital common ground that will provide miraculous breakthrough. Unexamined faith can only endure if Satan succeeds in confusing us. The Bible makes the appeal to examine our ways and test the essence of matters. It also instructs us to seek peace. This is doable. This is practical. Like the followers of God in the Book of Hebrews, faith is about trusting God about how to live. With a clear perspective of what faith is and how it works, I can put to rest my worries about religion because God is calling me to follow Him through faith. I trust God that His principles will secure me. Perhaps true Christianity is not religion at all, but rather a relationship with God.

The Kingdom of Heaven

This search has me on course to follow the Lord all the way through the gates of heaven. Jesus has the wheel and is steering me in the direction of His kingdom. In knowing what religion is truly supposed to be and how my faith works, God is able to show me what the kingdom of heaven looks like. Jesus spoke in many parables about His Kingdom, providing a handle to grasp—where, what, when, and the mystery of it:

"…The kingdom of heaven is at hand" (Matthew 10:7). "…What is the kingdom of God like, and to what shall I compare it?" (Luke 13:18). "…The kingdom of heaven is like a mustard seed, which a man took and sowed in his field; and this is smaller than all *other* seeds, but when it is full grown, it is larger than the garden plants and becomes a tree, so that THE BIRDS OF THE AIR COME AND NEST IN ITS BRANCHES" (Matthew 13:31-32).

"…The kingdom of God is like a man who cast seed upon the soil; and he goes to bed at night and gets up by day, and the seed sprouts and grows—how, he himself does not know. The soil produces crops by itself; first the blade, then the head, then the mature grain in the head. But when the crop permits, he immediately puts in the sickle, because the harvest has come" (Mark 4:26-29).

"…The kingdom of God is not coming with signs to be observed;

nor will they say, 'Look, here *it is*!' or, 'There *it is*!' For behold, the kingdom of God is in your midst" (Luke17:20-21). "…Truly I say to you, unless you are converted and become like children, you will not enter the kingdom of heaven. Whoever then humbles himself as this child, he is the greatest in the kingdom of heaven" (Matthew 18:3-4).

The kingdom of heaven is at hand. It provides covering. It grows mysteriously and will be harvested. It is humble, without show and exhibition. Jesus prayed that the will of God would "…be done, On earth as it is in heaven" (Matthew 6:10). The kingdom of God is in our midst. Jesus told His disciple Peter, "whatever you bind on earth shall have been bound in heaven, and whatever you loose on earth shall have been loosed in heaven" (Matthew 16:19). Perhaps God gives us the opportunity to make the kingdom everything He purposed it to be.

I've thought of God's kingdom as heaven, and heaven as a far off place in another dimension. I've thought of the earth realm as a place far removed from heaven and disconnected, but I'm reading that these two places aren't so detached or disengaged with one another. Rather, it seems as though God calls for the harmony of both. I can see the common sense of this since "…God created the heavens and the earth" (Genesis 1:1). So why would God want these realms disjoined? Jesus said to, "…receive the kingdom of God like a child…" (Mark 10:15), and also that, "…the kingdom of God is in your midst" (Luke 17:21). I am to receive the kingdom of God that is in my midst. I can know this kingdom because for those who know God in truth, "To you has been given the mystery of the kingdom of God" (Mark 4:11).

Jesus also said, "Truly, truly, I say to you, unless one is born again he cannot see the kingdom of God…Truly, truly, I say to you, unless one is born of water and the Spirit he cannot enter the kingdom of God. That which is born of the flesh is flesh, and that which is born of the Spirit is spirit" (John 3:3,5,6). This means I can also see the kingdom of God by accepting and receiving who Jesus is in my heart. This is what being "born again" means. If I understand correctly, my first birth was my natural birth from my mother. My second birth is the birth of my spirit realizing the truth about Jesus and committing my life to following Him.

Jesus asked His disciples, "…who do you say that I am?" (Matthew 16:15), and Peter professed to Jesus saying, "…You are the Christ, the Son of the living God. And Jesus said to him, 'Blessed are you, Simon Barjonah, because flesh and blood did not reveal *this* to you, but My Father who is in heaven. I also say to you that you are Peter, and upon this rock I will build My church; and the gates of Hades will not overpower it. I will give you the keys of the kingdom of heaven; and whatever you bind on earth shall have been bound in heaven, and whatever you loose on earth shall have been loosed in heaven" (Matthew 16:16-19).

By Peter realizing the truth about Jesus and professing in his heart and with his voice that Jesus is the Christ, he was born of the spirit. Peter was born again. So Jesus goes on to tell Peter that the church will be built upon this rock. The kingdom of God on earth starts with declaring who Jesus is. Within Peter's confession I've come to understand there are two schools of thought about who or what the "rock" is in this passage of scripture. One school says that Peter is the rock, the head of the church appointed by Jesus because he was given the keys of the kingdom of heaven. Hence, we have the Pope. The second school of thought says the rock is Peter's revelation of Jesus as the Christ, Christ being the fulfillment of prophecy. This would then be the rock of trust in Jesus, and this aspect would therefore be what God is building the kingdom upon.

A third school of thought would say it is both. I don't claim to know the absolute truth about the exact exchange between Peter and Jesus at that moment, but by my declaration of Jesus as Christ and revelation of who He is makes me born of the spirit. It means I have received the kingdom of God as a child—sincerely. It means the kingdom of God is in my midst—within me. All who belong to Jesus by way of revelation becomes the true magnitude of God's kingdom. The kingdom of God doesn't seem to be about one denomination or another, as long as the essential truth a denomination holds about God is doctrinally intact according to the Bible. It is very apparent that my life is connected and bound to heaven through my relationship with Jesus. It's culturally evident that our actions serve to bind or loose things in the earth realm, perhaps causing some kind of effect in heaven. God's kingdom is undoubtedly built upon all who will follow Jesus, which means the kingdom of God is here on earth, living through the Christ relationship, working through the sacrifice and power of Jesus—the rock of salvation undoubtedly starts with knowing and growing in Jesus.

I found another parable that illustrates how heaven has been visiting the earth and how we have been responding over time. It speaks of creation, stewardship, the need to hear what heaven is saying to earth, and what will ultimately occur based on what we've done with the situation:

"A man planted a vineyard and rented it out to vine-growers, and went on a journey for a long time. At the *harvest* time he sent a slave to the vine-growers, so that they would give him *some* of the produce of the vineyard; but the vine-growers beat him and sent him away empty-handed. And he proceeded to send another slave; and they beat him also and treated him shamefully and sent him away empty-handed. And he proceeded to send a third; and this one also they wounded and cast out. The owner of the vineyard said, 'What shall I do? I will send my beloved son; perhaps they will respect him.' But when the vine-growers saw him, they reasoned with one another, saying, 'This is the heir; let us kill him so that the inheritance will be ours.' So they threw him out of the vineyard and killed him. What, then, will the owner of the vineyard do to them? He will come and destroy these vine-growers and will give the vineyard to others" (Luke 20:9-16).

The "planting" is creation and we are its renters. God has left us to steward over the earth. The slaves are the prophets and signs God is speaking to us through, and yet we have not listened. The beloved son that was sent was Jesus, yet the earth realm rejected Him. God is set to destroy those who reject Christ whom He sent. This parable reveals the interaction between heaven and earth. It represents work and nurturing—a process meant to yield results. The kingdom of God means laboring together and respecting one another, and ultimately receiving Jesus. I conclude that although the kingdom of heaven is mysterious, it is nonetheless serious. It's so serious that I stop to wonder if the kingdom of God is something I could ever lose hold of. Is it possible for me to lose my salvation and be put out of the kingdom of heaven?

At the Heart of It All

Throughout the Bible, the main theme over and over is God's desire to be intimate with His creation—with you and me. I gather the same for you. At the end of a day, and especially the end of a life, God is by our side and wants us to be with Him.

> "…God our Savior…desires all…to be saved and to come to the knowledge of the truth" (1 Timothy 2:3-4).

Truth presents an opportunity for intimacy. Someone hoping for me to know truth, without malicious intent, represents love and compassion. I used to think people were trying to win me over to Christ just so I would be like them. Now I see that they are genuinely concerned for my eternal destiny. They know that only true intimacy with God leads to eternity. Only true intimacy with God will bring fulfillment to life here on earth. I'm convinced that God's ultimate purpose with His creation is love and intimacy with us. In the end, intimacy with God matters the most.

This being said, to me one of the most concerning verses in the Bible is when Jesus said, "Not everyone who says to Me, 'Lord, Lord,' will enter the kingdom of heaven, but he who does the will of My Father who is in heaven *will enter*. Many will say to Me on that day, 'Lord, Lord, did we not prophesy in Your name, and in Your name cast out demons, and in Your name perform many miracles?' And then I will declare to them, 'I never knew you; DEPART FROM ME, YOU WHO PRACTICE LAWLESSNESS'" (Matthew 7:21-23).

I profess Jesus as Lord and Savior, yet could God still reject me? I may not have cast out any demons or performed miracles that I know of, but I am willing to do what God planned for me. Could I still end up someone who says, "Lord, Lord," and be told by Jesus to depart? Though I examine my life and the Bible and have reassurance God will accept me, Matthew 7:21-23 is something I don't take lightly. After all, these are people who've *claimed* to know God, yet are turned away by God. How can "missing the point" about God be avoided—truly knowing God, God truly knowing us? Eternal life is not just another issue. It's the most valuable resource of all! I want to best understand how to hold on to God.

Since the solid ground of Matthew 7:24-27 we read earlier follows the passage of scripture we just read, it warrants reading again:

"Therefore everyone who hears these words of Mine and acts on them, may be compared to a wise man who built his house on the rock. And the rain fell, and the floods came, and the winds blew and slammed against that house; and *yet* it did not fall, for it had been founded on the rock. Everyone who hears these words of Mine and does not act on them, will be like a foolish man who built his house on the sand. The rain fell, and the floods came, and the winds blew and slammed against that house; and it fell—and great was its fall" (Matthew 7:24-27).

I need to break this down and grasp what Jesus means. The goal is to know God. So why would Jesus declare not to know someone who claims to know Him? This is my initial question. First, I see Jesus commending the wise person who hears His words and acts on them. I equate this to accurately hearing the words of Jesus through reading the Bible, also by hearing it's teaching by others. Jesus then says to act upon His words. John recorded Jesus as saying, "He who has My commandments and keeps them is the one who loves Me; and he who loves Me will be loved by My Father, and I will love him and will disclose Myself to him…If anyone loves Me, he will keep My word; and My Father will love him, and We will come to him and make Our abode with him" (John 14:21, 23).

So according to the words of the Bible, if I truly love God I will search to know the things Jesus said and will do them. Jesus had been approached about what someone can do to inherit eternal life:

"And someone came to Him and said, 'Teacher, what good thing shall I do that I may obtain eternal life?' And He said to Him, 'Why are you asking Me about what is good? There is *only* One who is good; but if you wish to enter into life, keep the commandments.' *Then* he said to Him, 'Which ones?' And Jesus said, 'YOU SHALL NOT COMMIT MURDER; YOU SHALL NOT COMMIT ADULTERY; YOU SHALL NOT STEAL; YOU SHALL NOT BEAR FALSE WITNESS; HONOR YOUR FATHER AND MOTHER; and YOU SHALL LOVE YOUR NEIGHBOR AS YOURSELF.' The young man said to Him, 'All these things I have kept; what am I still lacking?' Jesus said to him, 'If you wish to be complete, go *and* sell your possessions and give to *the* poor, and you will have treasure in heaven; and come, follow Me.' But when the young man heard this statement, he went away grieving; for he was one who owned much property. And Jesus said to His disciples, 'Truly I say to you, it is hard for a rich man to enter the kingdom of heaven. Again I say to you, it is easier for a camel to go through the eye of a needle, than for a rich man to enter the kingdom of God.' When His disciples heard *this*, they were very astonished and said, 'Then who can be saved?' And looking at *them* Jesus said to them, 'With people this is impossible, but with God all things are possible'" (Matthew 19:16-26).

In this young man's mind he *was* indeed following God, but after talking with Jesus he was troubled. Jesus challenged his heart as to the hold he had on his possessions, and that it could keep any one of us from following God through the gates of eternity. Jesus therefore told him to go and sell and give to the poor. I also don't find Jesus saying that wealth is evil or sinful, or that being rich means going to hell. Who can even say this young man is not with Jesus this day? Jesus *was* saying worldly wealth has the power to distract our hearts away from God. One of the hardest things for me to do would be to give everything I worked for to people who are poor. I can only imagine what went through the young man's head. The point I gather from their exchange and what I know is in the Bible is that I'm to be careful not to clutch on to the things pulling my heart away from God, since the most important thing ever is for my heart to be with God.

When Jesus said it is easier for a camel to go through the eye of a needle, I learn He was referring to the entry point through the wall of a city back in His day. The eye of the needle was an opening in a city wall, tall and wide enough for a camel to go through. However, it did not leave much room for a camel fully loaded with ones possessions to easily fit through. History describes the times when people would be seen offloading their camel so they could fit through the wall, pulling their stuff through after and entering into the city. The parallel I see Jesus drawing is between fitting through the eye of the needle and entering heaven. I should be able to let go of anything I carry that could keep my soul from fitting through to His presence. The question is am I willing to let go? Nothing is greater than God, yet I wrestle God for the things that may ultimately separate me from Him. This is not God's desire.

The rich young ruler approaching Jesus had a tight hold on his possessions. It's understandable. It's so hard not to—whether with little or with much. I need to check my grip on things and make sure it's loose enough for God to break. I've got to be able to hold onto God. If I assume wealth and possessions are evil, I miss the point here. I used to think the Bible said, "Money is the root to all evil." I've learned it doesn't. The Bible says in 1 Timothy 6:10: "…the love of money is a root of all sorts of evil…" It's the *love* of money that gets us. Satan would have us believe money is evil and that poverty is one of the greatest virtues. I'm sure Satan prefers that God's people be less empowered than God actually intends. Timothy went on to write, "…and some by for it [money] have wandered away from the faith and pierced themselves with many griefs" (1 Timothy 6:10). Money is not evil. It's my love and longing for it that will pull me away from God.

Even Jesus had wealthy friends who were generous and who knew and believed in God, and their relationship was right with God. It's not about *things*. It's about the heart. Jesus spoke more times about our relationship with money than just about anything else. He knows we stumble over the issue of money. The Bible makes it clear I must accept Jesus as true, follow after Him, keep the commandments, repent for disobeying His ways, and seek forgiveness from God. All the while, doing my absolute best to love God with everything I have and am. I trust that truly knowing God means doing everything in my power to in fact, know God. What more can I do? Nothing.

As I search the Scriptures I find the way to God and eternal life—through Christ. Jesus then leads me through a life-long process devoted to knowing God and desiring to do the will of God. I do see that failing is inevitable—falling short of God's commandments and Law. This is evident in my life and explained in the Bible. I don't see some kind of magic formula that should make us think, "I've already made it to heaven on this side of life because I believe in Jesus. I'm done now." I see that humility is the calling. There is instruction to, "…clothe yourselves with humility toward one another, for GOD IS OPPOSED TO THE PROUD, BUT GIVES GRACE TO THE HUMBLE. Therefore humble yourselves under the mighty hand of God, that He may exalt you at the proper time, casting all your anxiety on Him, because He cares for you" (1 Peter 5:5-7).

When I am weak, there are others around me who can help and support my walk with The Lord, because God does not intend me to walk alone. We are called to work out the things of God together. The goal I see is never giving up on following God. For this I will know God, and God me. I find no simple answer for what it means to know God. There are indications that knowing God is a forward-looking process. "…No one, after putting his hand to the plow and looking back, is fit for the kingdom of God" (Luke 9:62). It's difficult to say at exactly which point someone who follows Jesus looks back and becomes unfit for God's kingdom. It's much easier to accept God's grace as truly incomprehensible. The most important key is my decision to follow Jesus and continue in it.

From here, all I can really do is continuously pursue after God and leave my old self and ways behind. No matter how aged I get, this journey to know God should never end. And maybe it's the day my seeking might end that becomes the day I stop knowing God. Perhaps it's this simple, and perhaps I should not let worry eat at me, because trusting God is the most powerful way to know God. I admit that I still wrestle with things, but I do see that the most important thing for me to do is to trust God and His promises. I'm starting to recognize that every aspect of God's intervention into the human experience is designed to draw us deeper into intimacy with Him so that we will know Him. Intimacy is God's greatest desire. For that reason God invites everyone to nestle up to Him, with open hearts that we may speak to God not only as God, but also as friend. The presence of God is a warm, secure place—life and hope. The comfort of the Spirit is a soothing womb, surrounding my very being. Grace cultivates deep intimacy between the Creator and the creation. This is where I want to be.

Where the Bible says, "…become like children…Whoever then humbles himself as this child, he is the greatest in the kingdom of heaven" (Matthew 18:3-4), and "…for the kingdom of heaven belongs to such as these" (Matthew 19:14); I focus on being a little child before Him, without guile, sincerely seeking the heart of Jesus who restores the innocence to my soul. This sustained voyage of vulnerability is something I intimately travel with the Holy Spirit. The full blessing may very well be never quite arriving at any particular place, but a constant journey walked eternally with God, forever drawing me, forever loving me. I gather this is what it means to know God. This is the heart of God that I pursue Him.

It's my opinion that it would be impolite at the very least to go on living without acknowledging the presence of God. How would any one of us respond if over and over again we hosted someone in our home, they came to eat our food, and recline on our sofa, and received all the blessings our home offered, only to find they really didn't care to know us at all, or even our name? Eventually who would invite this person back into their home? I think after a while I'd get the hint that this person has rejected me. I would have trouble leaving the door open to them. I know you can relate.

Perhaps God may look at us in a similar way. God gives life and offers it eternally. By God allowing entrance into the presence of heaven through Jesus, I see this as God wanting us to know Himself, and also understanding why I would be granted the priceless gift of eternity. Not wanting to know whom my breath comes from may exhibit disrespect for God. Perhaps we play a role in casting ourselves from the presence of God for the simple lack of acknowledgement of God's presence. So may I live to respect and honor God for the life I have.

Destiny

We have many questions about our individual destinies and purposes. My burden to know my own has been relentless. I understand who God is and now have a relationship with Jesus. I am aware of the battle between good and evil, and prepare my self within it. Through this, God is leading me to see my purpose. Though, the only detailed map I see specifically charting my life is the one following me. I know God sees it all, but requires me to walk in faith. How long will I be doing what I'm doing at my job, or at school? Being a single man, does God want me to some day marry? Where will I be living ten years from now? Will my body stay healthy? How can I truly know in which direction to walk? Being brought to this image upon Half Dome helped me begin grasping my purpose. Diligent study of this sign and the Bible leads me to become conscious of my destiny. There is now so much more clarity where before there wasn't, and as I keep pressing into my relationship with God I suddenly find myself in the midst of my purposes.

I've been led to these very pages to write about reality and help supply understanding about the nature of truth and how it points to Jesus. The sign on Half Dome has encouraged me to learn of all these important aspects of life I now write about. God, family, and truth are of paramount importance. I now look at my relationship with them as major priorities in fulfilling my destiny. My family and friends are now seen as integral parts of who I am and everything I am to become. Self was the focus, but now self is being put in its rightful place.

In the past a faulty premise of reality kept me from knowing my purpose. My destiny was riddled with uncertainty because I was not appraising life accurately. This caused conflict and frustration within me. It muddied my vision to the point of not being able to see. How could I truly know all that is in me if I don't really know God, denying Jesus? I was greatly limited in knowing my potential, let alone fulfilling it. But once I saw what God had done on the granite mountain, clues and answers were found—direction was given through the Bible. By knowing God, my own soul in turn, is being revealed to me.

Do I know one hundred percent everything about my purpose and destiny? I don't know if I ever will, but rich vision now courses through my spirit and working to see it through will consume the rest of my days. The biggest clue to my inspiration and purpose are my gifts and the people and situations now part of my life—what God has given, and continues giving to me. The more I practically understand this the more my purpose becomes clear. Knowing it comes by way of realizing my gifts and the things God appoints me to steward.

The way I begin filling in the blanks about my destiny is by starting with the gifts of God. I see answers stemming from the greatest gift—life. This is my first gift. The greatest gift for life in a sinful predicament becomes salvation—my second gift. "For by grace you have been saved through faith; and that not of yourselves, *it is* the gift of God" (Ephesians 2:8). This verse tells me salvation is a gift of grace. "...Repent, and each of you be baptized in the name of Jesus Christ for the forgiveness of your sins; and you will receive the gift of the Holy Spirit. For the promise is for you and your children and for all who are far off, as many as the Lord our God will call to Himself" (Acts 2:38-39). These verses explain there is an indwelling Spirit of God within me when I walk with Christ. It is the gift of the Holy Spirit given through receiving salvation from Christ. "For the wages of sin is death, but the free gift of God is eternal life in Christ Jesus our Lord" (Romans 6:23). Life is the primary gift and now because of sin, salvation becomes equally important. Understanding the gift of life and Christ's gift of salvation opened the window of my spirit to see so much more of whom I am destined to be. This led to recognizing my other gifts.

"Every good thing given and every perfect gift is from above, coming down from the Father of lights, with whom there is no variation or shifting shadow" (James 1:17). God does not hold back gifts from anyone for any reason. God gives to all, inherently, "For there is no partiality with God" (Roman 2:11). God gives gifts to me regardless of who I am. By this I know there are gifts in me to find and cultivate. I seek God to know my gifts and work to develop them. There is no good reason for them to remain hidden in me. It would be tragic to never know or use my God-given gifts. God has put gifts in everyone.

My gifts are personalized. The Bible teaches that each person "…has his own gift from God, one in this manner, and another in that" (1 Corinthians 7:7). "As each one has received a *special* gift, employ it in serving one another as good stewards of the manifold grace of God" (1 Peter 4:10). This confirms the responsibility to steward my traits, gifts, and talents. Now, it becomes a process to identify and learn how to use them.

Jesus told a story relating to gifts, or talents. Back in Jesus' day, talent was money. Today, talent is thought of as a person's ability. This parable starting at Matthew 25:14 illustrates that talents are given from a supreme authority. The parable shows that talents are given to each person according to their willingness to steward them. It demonstrates that God gives talents and expects us to use and apply, to cultivate and grow them, but not to hide away in fear. Jesus' conclusion was, "For to everyone who has, *more* shall be given, and he will have an abundance; but from the one who does not have, even what he does have shall be taken away" (Matthew 25:29). I think of this principal as "use or lose."

This parable tells me about the nature of God's gifts. If I don't talk, my speech doesn't develop. If I don't use my muscles, they atrophy. If I don't practice love, love will not be in me. If not growing, I'm dying. Not using my spiritual gifts and talents given by God results in their withering away.

Writing and having deep discussions about cultural issues are beginning to surface as my natural gifts. Working with my hands building to create things are also part of who I am. Thoroughly conveying information to other people is also a talent I'm beginning to develop. In the construction industry information is vital. I've learned the hard way that clear communication helps to get something done right the first time. As I use these gifts and talents, my life purposes are being fulfilled. These gifts define and steer me. I feel like I'm finally becoming me. It sounds a little strange, but I sense my soul is awakening to its true self. The self inside asking to be fulfilled is beginning to manifest. As I develop my gifts, more of my purpose becomes clear. As more of my purpose becomes clear, so do more of my gifts. The synergistic relationship between my gifts and purpose are revealing my destiny. The closer to God I get, the more developed the gifts become, the clearer my purpose and destiny is evident.

The biggest clue to knowing my destiny comes when I ask, "Before I die what are the most important things I need to do here on earth?" Part of the answer is clear: knowing Jesus. This relationship shadows everything, because eternal life not secured while alive only puts off the coming wrath and judgment. Therefore, the single most vital aspect of life is obtaining the gift of salvation through Christ.

A big part of my purpose becomes sharing life with others. If I stay true to my gifts they will guide me in the ways I am to make known the reality of God to others. For any one of us it could be through benevolence, music, art, speaking, writing, but most importantly—doing it no matter what my job is, in an excellent manner. Even running a business with the heart of God is of great magnitude. You name it. By staying true to my gifts, in turn I see other parts of my purpose fall into place. The primary purpose is to seek salvation in Jesus, and the secondary purpose to be witness of Jesus. I start by loving my family first.

The Bible instructs me to care for my family, because "…if anyone does not provide for his own, and especially for those of his household, he has denied the faith…" (1 Timothy 5:8). To neglect my family is to reject the truth. If God so blesses me with a wife and children in the future, there is no justification for me not to fully provide for them—food, shelter, *and* love. We're thinking, "This is common sense," but then we know or hear about so many broken homes, physical abuse, and blatant rejection of children. So maybe this common sense is not as commonly practiced. This means there are too many people neglecting God's intended destiny for their life. The next giant clue to knowing my personal purposes and destiny centers on the family.

I am called by God to love my mother and father, or those who've raised me. I see this as "honoring my mother and father" written in the Ten Commandments. Say my father has rejected me in some ways. I can either overcome and be healed from his neglect by forgiving him or him hopefully loving me, or struggle indefinitely over being rejected by another human being. This is a tough spot for both people. The preventative solution to this predicament is choosing not to reject people in the first place. If I ever make the choice to start a family of my own, I'm required to provide, care for, and love my children and my wife—this principle reinforced by God. Flat-out abandoning them is in no way a Godly option, regardless of what my feelings may lead me to do. Family desertion is immoral. It is a lie from hell if I tell myself otherwise. Therefore, by choosing to start a family, my family automatically becomes a major, major, major part of my purpose and destiny. Did I mention major? It's supposed to consume me in the best possible ways. It's honorable. If I don't get this right, my destiny in God will get put on hold. Let's look at this a little closer.

There is too much divorce and neglect around me, and I see self-pride keeping people apart—a negative kind of pride. Our self-importance and selfishness is what should be abandoned instead of the family. The hearts of fathers need to be restored to their children through the Spirit of Christ. Children's hearts need to be restored to their fathers and mothers. Too many fathers are abandoning their family, leaving the mother and children to struggle. This is not God's destiny for anyone, which is a vital clue about what a person's destiny is *not*. Family abandonment is not part of God's plan for our life. The catastrophic neglect and abandonment of children by their parents produce a battlefield of dead and broken purposes that then curse the next generation born into it. Satan then beats us over the head with guilt and shame, serving to paralyze our destinies in God. It's so vital to comprehend that family neglect seeks to steal our Godly destiny.

Our destinies demand that parents are praying for each other, that fathers and mothers would have a loving heart for their children. It's so easy to see how I could get off course with my life by neglecting this significant part of my destiny. Love and restoration are duties, not options. I have a great sense that God will bless my destiny through my faithfulness to steward it properly. Practically, this amounts to being responsible with my relationships and working at fulfilling the needs of them.

The harshest cases of neglect are when babies are physically neglected. They are perfectly helpless people we bring into the world, who depend on parents to nurture and keep them alive. It's beyond words to describe the tragedies when babies are left to suffer. But the world manages to top this neglectful condition by killing unborn life in the mother's womb because parents lack the commitment to care for it. A person's destiny is virtually eliminated to avoid any *assumed* inconvenience or challenge. Two things here about why this is happening: either we're not trusting God with our destiny, or we're not pursuing our destiny in God. An expectant mother whose life proves to be threatened with a perilous predicament is about the only circumstance where removing her unborn baby should even be considered to save her. Limiting the termination of a pregnancy to this kind of special circumstance would make it altogether a rare incidence. We're talking about the annihilation of a growing life because parents aren't willing to commit to raising another person. How is this selfish act a Godly principle? We took on the risk of getting pregnant through the choice to have sex. The extreme neglect of human life proliferating throughout the globe holds the world back from fulfilling its God-given purposes. We must do better than this.

If I factor out my obligations to my family I automatically fail to fulfill my purpose on earth. The life I bring into this world becomes a mighty part of my purpose. If we abandon people we're responsible for we literally grab for something that is not ours. This should warn me that I'm choosing to let go of my destiny in God. Purposes and responsibilities are intertwined. If one day I have children and impart major dysfunction and emotional handicaps, they start off struggling unnecessarily to know their purposes and may lose sight of their destiny right off the bat. It's not in God's purpose for me to leave a legacy of confusion and frustration that may even have them hating God for reasons I impose. As a whole, the world is negatively affected when we fail to know and fulfill our purposes. Even financial debt has the power to shackle those in it with anxiety and monetary burdens. We actually limit ourselves from being able to help our family and others the way we sense God leading us to. It's also not to say that hardships and obstacles won't be overcome in the face of daunting circumstances. It's proven they can be. Our disobedience to God will always be the biggest obstacle in our way. Perhaps through our obedience to the principles of God and the Holy Spirit we will limit the many obstructions in our way. I believe we could be excelling to heights we've not begun to imagine.

Purpose and destiny are indeed heavy subjects. Our personal destinies affect each other. I'm encouraged to faithfully fulfill my own so that I may also see others fulfilled. Continuing to recognize my God-given gifts sets me in the direction to fulfill my purposes. Things that energize me tell me how I'm designed. When I write, deliberate issues with others, or even build things with my hands, I feel charged. Things that drain or tire me are typically not my gift. I think of administration needs, or working on my car. It's not that I won't do them. I just know they're not my strengths. I'd much rather be out talking to people about interesting projects.

What is it for you? Is it managing finances or people, is it promoting a product? How about sewing, or cooking, or raising children? When you talk about something specific do your particles charge up? Is it law enforcement, or maybe civil leadership? Could it be designing components that advance us technologically? Farmers, bakers, barbers, carpenters, clerks, counselors, doctors or nurses; fishermen, lawyers or judges, musicians, preachers, soldiers, tax collectors, teachers, or writers—all are worthy callings and carried out with passion when done out of our God-given talent. Our unique, innate abilities enhance our performance when we recognize and develop them.

We are all called to be stewards over the talents God gave to us. The challenge is getting to the bottom of who we really are inside. From me to you, your talents could be anything, but between you and God they can be determined. One thing is certain, when I'm not operating according to my God-given talents and purposes tension abides within me, even between others and me. It may not always be a conscious observation, but the call to fulfill what God put in me wants to be heard through the acts of me doing them. It's easy to get aggravated when I neglect my gifts and calling, because I innately sense something's missing or being mismanaged.

It's our mission to find out what we're on earth to do. It tears at us until we resolve it. Writing this book is a big part of my destiny in God. This process with the Lord reveals more and more of my purpose each day. There is tremendous excitement about the things God will continue revealing. The more I work to understand my gifts, the clearer they become. We've been fortunate if we have loving and supportive parents that help us recognize and cultivate our God-given talents. Some of us are not so fortunate and have struggled, or struggle endlessly to have them revealed. In whatever stage we find ourselves, the Holy Spirit is by our side waiting to reveal the things of God.

No matter how physically or otherwise challenged we believe ourselves to be, our life is valuable. I'm speaking to you who've been dealt major, physical challenges. Whether you have hands or not, whether your limbs are different, or body not easy to move, the world needs your gifts to do what God is calling you to do through your challenges. Even disfigured, your life is meant to help others see true beauty, especially the miracles of God. Your presence makes the world a better place. Despite what anyone thinks or says or even how you may feel, without you the world would miss a tremendous blessing—immeasurable! Even God wants to bless others through you. Part of your purpose and mission is to teach souls. Crippled, diseased, or dying—it is obvious God imparts heavenly wisdom amidst the challenges of your struggle. In more ways than one, you reach the truest potential of life in light of daunting circumstances as you face your circumstances head-on. The world is powerfully reminded of true love and patience through those who endure—all the more when done with joy. You are soul teachers who are able to tap deep within the spirits of others and demonstrate the true meaning of life.

Not only have I witnessed the great physical challenges of others, my brother Adam has cerebral palsy and is captive in a wheelchair struggling to communicate his needs. I witness the power of God through his life. Our family and others around Adam choose to rise to the occasion, meeting his needs of care and love. As a result, I see the hand of God surrounding his life and touching those who are near him. My mom and dad are powerful examples of God's great mercy. One of Adam's purposes is to bring out the best in others and remind us that life comes in all shapes and sizes. Adam is just as valuable as anyone else. As he depends on others, others depend on Adam, and everyone becomes more of who God made them to be. Since birth, my brother Adam from his wheel chair continues to be an inspiration to our family and many others.

I plan on being used by God, and utilize my resources to obtain what is necessary to fulfill my purposes. Little by little I build my skills, cultivate my relationships, and position my life to partner with God. It's shaping up to be a lifelong process to accomplish my purposes, but I also can't assume I've got a full life span to get things right. Focusing on God's plan this day is therefore prudent. The Bible lets me know that, "The plans of the diligent *lead* surely to advantage, But everyone who is hasty *comes* surely to poverty" (Proverbs 21:5).

The Apostle Paul encourages me by writing, "*I pray that* the eyes of your heart may be enlightened, so that you will know what is the hope of His calling, what are the riches of the glory of His inheritance in the saints, and what is the surpassing greatness of His power toward us who believe…" (Ephesians 1:18-19). How I live out the rest of my time on earth matters to the highest degree.

I'm learning how to balance the fulfillment of my purposes with everyday life. It's amazing how God makes time for the things He wants me to do. I used to think that being successful at my job meant having to sacrifice profane amounts of time away from friends and family. I'm relieved to learn that God isn't calling me to neglect them in order to fulfill my destiny. I thought otherwise because of wanting a certain lifestyle. What would it take? Another deal, a better position, and more hours for more money? Personal responsibilities and higher calling can be tough to balance, but it all boils down to trusting God to live according to Biblical principles.

The implication of God's morality and the obligation to have integrity has turned into a natural progression, directing me to know about the wrath of the Almighty and how to have a healthy fear of God. I've been encouraged to understand God's justice and how to have a relationship with Christ. The sign on Half Dome sparked an explosion of answers that began a chain reaction of truth. God is seen in remarkable ways, helping me to make sense of both religion and faith. The kingdom of God is showing itself to be very real. At the heart of it all I see God intimately calling me that my destiny would be fulfilled.

What we choose to do about all of this is in our hands. God has laid out the tools for victory in the battle between good and evil. How will we respond? The rest amounts to living out the principles of God while anticipating the return of Christ. Jesus prayed,

"…Our Father who is in heaven, hallowed be Your name. Your kingdom come. Your will be done, On earth as it is in heaven. Give us this day our daily bread. And forgive us our debts, as we also have forgiven our debtors. And do not lead us into temptation, but deliver us from evil" (Matthew 6:9-14).

<u>Chapter Seven</u>

The Time

"Breathe. Let go. And remind yourself that this very moment
is the only one you know you have for sure."
– Oprah Winfrey

With the slight red tint now dominating the sky, the sea rising and the swells picking up, a knock at the door has gotten my attention. When I opened the door people were lined up outside. They apparently wanted to come in to this old, weathered house. They are all very calm and just seem to be waiting. I looked back into the small living room and wonder how they are all going to fit in here. Even so, I step aside and put my hand out as a gesture to say, "Make your self comfortable." Each one enters. Then I turned to see a ladder in the middle of the room. It leads up to what typically would be an attic, yet I can see the blue sky and clouds through this three foot by three foot square opening. The first person walks past me into the house toward the ladder, the others follow in the same direction. I watch the first one reach the top and begin to step into where ever the ladder is leading. It is at this moment I awake from this dream, and began to process it.

This is still that same dream of mine, which came to me shortly after my very first encounter in Yosemite. It's the same one with the massive rock hovering in the sky, with the seven descending volts of cloud, the unusual aspect of some seeing and some not seeing the event, the multitudes of people roaming about, the old house, the rising sea and marching swells, and the ladder reaching through the ceiling toward the sky—and in this dream these events are preceded with that perfect, ordinary day like any other. I'm still not exactly sure about what to fully make of this whole dream yet. I know it's as vivid in my mind as it was the day I awoke from it. Perhaps some day I will be able to entirely grasp what it represents. For today though, questions remain.

Prevail of Peace

Aren't we tired of the lines separating us—our political affiliations, our spirituality? Consider the world being set free of its immoral poverty and sufferings by uniting in truth. Could it ever actually happen? The whole point of living, aside from loving and helping others, is to know and adore God. My story among the multitude is just about someone who deeply desired to know the truth whether God existed or not. I fought off being deceived by my own philosophical desires. I wanted to know my true origin. I figured this would be the starting point of how to live: if no God, then my life is my own to do whatever I please. But since God revealed Himself to me He expects greater things of me.

So I ask, "What should be done with all these universal facts? How can we ignore God pointing to Jesus, and the shout of God so obviously displayed on Half Dome?" We've got to acknowledge it! How could we somehow sweep this revelation of truth under the rug and pretend as though we are not witnessing reality? These are valid questions for people to answer within their own heart. The one thing I am very concerned about is if we individually choose not to answer God in kind.

I'm simply reporting a discovery, which I'm finding is really turning out to be a "rediscovery." This is not about even agreeing with me. It's about agreeing with God. It's about holding onto truth and letting go of that which keeps us from Christ. I wish I had a simple answer. I wish I could walk through our tough choices together about what ideas and traditions to keep and what to set aside. But I do know that the Spirit of God will help us make the right choices. We just need to trust God to lead us.

Knowing the truth about reality is so much more than a feeling, a fire in the belly, an experience, or a story handed down—it is even more than a fact. It's everything combined. We are alive because God made our heart to beat, pumping blood through our body to our brain that commands our very being to function. A body without a brain will not enable the heart to deliver its life, nor will a body survive without its network. So it is the same with truth as it forms reality. Each fact, feeling, experience, and account manifests a picture. Each piece makes up the whole part. The world needs to be courageous enough to identify what is real and challenge what is not. We need to be strong and not take the compilation of truth personally, or as an insult. It is not about being wrong—it is about seeing reality as it is.

If you feel that truth is not represented here go and set the record straight. Offense need not be taken and the consideration of truth need not be refused. If one's pursuit becomes an argument for the purpose of soothing some offense taken, rather than considering the truth, then woe to the pursuit. I hope to see the day when truth prevails over pride. So why does it matter what the truth ends up being anyway? It is what it is—nothing more, nothing less. It's not personal and it's no one's fault. We have to get over the "worldview shopping" tendencies, taking a little bit of this and a little bit of that until we think our cart is full enough. I don't see reality as giving us the option to shop for notions. I see searching as a purpose to uncover life's essence to accept and receive. There's a prayer that goes like this: "God grant me the serenity to accept the things I cannot change, the courage to change the things I can, and the wisdom to know the difference." This is what I'm talking about.

Who doesn't agree that knowing the truth is primary? If truth is treated as secondary then we've identified an agenda with some major concerns. It's fundamentally problematic to base our lives on anything other than what is true. A faulty foundation will systemically impact the world in negative ways. We are truly doomed if we cannot arrive to a common ground, mutual observance of truth and reality. It's not a human being's place to physically eliminate everyone or anything expressing an opposing worldview to his or her own. God has reserved this right for Himself if God so chooses to do so. We are to, "Depart from evil and do good; Seek peace and pursue it" (Psalm 34:14), and, "…be at peace with one another" (Mark 9:50).

The Bible lays out principles for pursuing peace. "So then we pursue the things which make for peace and the building up of one another" (Romans 14:19). We're to walk "…with all humility and gentleness, with patience, showing tolerance for one another in love, being diligent to preserve the unity of the Spirit in the bond of peace" (Ephesians 4:2-3). "Pursue peace with all men, and the sanctification without which no one will see the Lord" (Hebrews 12:14). "Never pay back evil for evil to anyone. Respect what is right in the sight of all men. If possible, so far as it depends on you, be at peace with all men. Never take your own revenge, beloved, but leave room for the wrath *of God*, for it is written, 'VENGEANCE IS MINE, I WILL REPAY,' says the Lord" (Romans 12:17-19).

Peace is ours to pursue. And even though Satan the adversary may not desire peace, we can be the ones to pursue it still. We've got to make a commitment to putting objective truth first above our personal agendas, above our hopes, even above our fears. The unity of all people is only attained under the reality of God. The Lord is offering to guide us in making the best personal and national decisions for our homes and the world.

Every corner of this globe has a chance to make our world the place God desires. God will thrust the world into a realm not yet seen or experienced when personal focus changes from pursuing vanity to pursuing God in truth. It's a positive act to beckon for the kingdom of God to come, calling for heaven to be manifested on earth. This means forgiving others while helping others, with the hope that those who are helped will one day help others in turn. Through Christ we can find the wherewithal to help the young from stumbling by promoting decency and justice. Most of all, we are ultimately led to God where we will truly know God and all that is in store for our lives. The wrath of God can be diverted from us by choosing Christ. The gaps of division can be bridged with truth and unity. This is the common ground set before us to walk upon together.

Life on earth is not intended by God to be about power, fame, or riches. The real achievement in the sight of God is, "…that we may lead a tranquil and quiet life in all godliness and dignity" (1 Timothy 2:2). This is what we should be shooting for. I never really thought this was the goal of living, but it makes all the sense. This, however, depends upon each person's commitment to giving off peace, representing peace, and wanting peace. Achieving peace is accomplished through knowing truth and proceeding to work together based on reality and justice, having mercy wherever possible. It can't begin to happen without knowing Jesus in heart.

It is written that eventually nations, "…will hammer their swords into plowshares and their spears into pruning hooks. Nation will not lift sword up against nation, And never again will they learn war" (Isaiah 2:4). Perfect peace can only come from God. Perfect peace will one day prevail. God will reconcile the gross disorder and injustices. We can be sure. In the meantime, we are not given the right to give up on peace. We are to know truth and pursue peace. This is God's desire.

Truth is the pathway to peace and freedom. In knowing the truth, "…the truth will make you free" (John 8:32). Knowing Jesus is "…the way, and the truth, and the life…" (John 14:6), and "…grace and truth were realized through Jesus Christ" (John 1:17). Peace with God and with each other can be established. On the part of everyone, we must work and pray for peace. The Holy Bible is the light in darkness with Jesus leading the way. The Bible speaks of so many ways peace is made.

"Depart from evil and do good; Seek peace and pursue it" (Psalm 34:14). God "…made peace through the blood of His cross…" (Colossians 1:20), "…having been justified by faith, we have peace with God through our Lord Jesus Christ" (Romans 5:1). "Let the peace of Christ rule in your hearts…" (Colossians 3:15). "Be anxious for nothing, but in everything by prayer and supplication with thanksgiving let your requests be made known to God. And the peace of God, which surpasses all comprehension, will guard your hearts and your minds in Christ Jesus" (Philippians 4:6-7). "For the mind set on the flesh is death, but the mind set on the Spirit is life and peace" (Romans 8:6). "…God is not *a God* of confusion but of peace…" (1 Corinthians 14:33). "[F]or the kingdom of God is not eating and drinking, but righteousness and peace and joy in the Holy Spirit. For he who in this *way* serves Christ is acceptable to God and approved by men. So then we pursue the things which make for peace and the building up of one another" (Romans 14:17-19). "Pursue peace with all men…" (Hebrews 12:14), because, "…God has called us to peace" (I Corinthians 7:15). By knowing and living this truth, peace will prevail. The question is not can we make peace; the question is will we?

There are so many worthy things to pursue that cultivate peace. Sacrificial actions make for peace. I am deeply touched when a movie or television program portrays miracles, and even deeper when it happens for real. I think of a reality television program in particular, who's in the business of interceding people's lives to meet great needs by reconstructing a new home and providing a family in great need with fresh start. Immense pushes of encouragement are exemplified—financially and spiritually. This is reality television at its best. It powerfully inspires me beyond words to witness these tremendous acts of kindness toward people in great need. It's inspiring to witness people who focus their lives on helping others. They lay aside vain pursuits of material wealth to build up others. That's the heart of Christ.

I saw a program on television where people had adopted children whom others had blatantly rejected. This new family gave them hope and a renewed vision for their destiny. It's difficult to even begin comprehending the humble spirit of people who make these kinds of sacrifices. I also saw a camp set up for children who have great physical and neurological challenges, many with life-threatening disease; bringing hope and encouragement to them by helping them to experience a time of freedom and adventure. In turn, these very children and young adults inspire us tenfold with their pure hearts and Godly insight to life itself. These are people who are answering their call from God. They are doing what they were born to do. Their destiny is being fulfilled. They are helping to bring the peace of God into our world.

People and places like these serve to "...encourage...all with resolute heart to remain *true* to the Lord; for he was a good man, and full of the Holy Spirit and of faith. And considerable numbers were brought to the Lord" (Acts 11:23-24). "He" was Barnabas. The Apostles called him Barnabas because it means, "...Son of Encouragement" (Acts 4:36). Such people and places of blessing represent the spirit of Barnabas, where the dreams of little ones who struggle so deeply are fulfilled as they partake in things they could only imagine. Who can argue these true miracles! This is God, working miracles through people who are willing to live the destiny God has for them. I want this! I want to do the things I was made to do and witness miracles working through my life. The Lord's great love allows people to be a part of the miraculous. God is inviting people to partake in great blessing and power. These are some of the choices made that promote peace.

Perhaps I've somewhat misunderstood the way of God's most common miracles, if miracles could ever be considered common. Before I understood God's relationship with us and our relationship with each other, I looked for "supernatural miracles" to help me witness God. Now, I'm learning that God prefers the humble path over a grand show; the intimate touch rather than a distant, miraculous shove. I better understand that God works much more through love and compassion at the human level, inviting and allowing people to play a holy role in the miraculous along with Him. Jesus having been born in a manger demonstrates the humilty of

God. Perhaps a grand display of the supernatural, such as this sign on Half Dome flows out of God's mercy to soothe our own insecurites and doubts. God seeks to accomplish His will through and with others, for others, rather than accomplishing everything on His own. He could, but a team effort displays the undeniable miracle of love and unity. Peace is manifested. As of now, the world's "idea" of God does not fully align with the "reality" of God, and so we struggle in tension while suffering continues, the world producing strife instead of peace. It doesn't have to be this way.

May God bless all who take the risks and make the sacrifices to create positive circumstances in people's lives. This is the work of angels on earth. May all who labor in love truly know God and possess His eternal blessing. I am so deeply affected by the way people choose to bless others for their demonstrated devotions of kindness. Volunteering to build new homes and new lives, sharing wealth and resources, bringing people together—all speak of great love and miracles. This part of our culture should be continuously promoted. Let it shine forth brighter and brighter, even more than the sun that we may see the true heart of God and follow it. We have the opportunity in Christ to make peace with each other and bless one another.

Yet I stop to consider I may be too hopeful here. Part of me can't help wondering about Christians who have major differences, who battle each other for power and influence. Abortion is one issue where civic leaders profess to be Christian, yet stand on opposite sides of this issue. Peace between the two is absent, yet both will say they are Christian. One calls it choice and the other murder. Why is this conflict unresolved? There's got to be a solution.

I'm reminded of instances throughout history where Christians violently fought each other. Violence among people who claim to follow Jesus even exists to this day. On one hand I read through the Bible and become inspired, but then on the other I look at the world and become discouraged. Maybe my hope of how the world can work together is too "unreal." Perhaps we're doomed and the fulfillment of prophecy's atrociousness will be brought about by our own self-imposed destruction. Then again, maybe the plan of Satan is to get the world thinking it's hopeless. One thing is for sure: I am looking to God for a miracle to help us. Perhaps this is the day we reconcile with one another, but what then if we give up? We can't. We shouldn't. God isn't giving us the option to quit.

Is Now the End?

Has the final Day of Judgment reached our doorstep? Could God be about to change planet earth, as we know it? I'm wondering what I should be hoping for—God to come and bring the new promised realm, or for more time to reconcile our situation. My ultimate hope is for peace on earth. At the same time I know that God is in control of the future. The revelation upon Half Dome stirs me to wonder what God is doing on earth at this point in time. I know the prophecies of the Bible explain some things. But what exactly is said and how simple is it to understand? Where are we at in God's schedule?

"…[L]et this be known to you and give heed to my words…this is what was spoken of through the prophet Joel: 'AND IT SHALL BE IN THE LAST DAYS,' God says, 'THAT I WILL POUR FORTH OF MY SPIRIT ON ALL MANKIND; AND YOUR SONS AND YOUR DAUGHTERS SHALL PROPHESY, AND YOUR YOUNG MEN SHALL SEE VISIONS, AND YOUR OLD MEN SHALL DREAM DREAMS; EVEN ON MY BONDSLAVES, BOTH MEN AND WOMEN, I WILL IN THOSE DAYS POUR FORTH OF MY SPIRIT,' And they shall prophesy. 'AND I WILL GRANT WONDERS IN THE SKY ABOVE AND SIGNS ON THE EARTH BELOW, BLOOD, AND FIRE, AND VAPOR OF SMOKE. THE SUN WILL BE TURNED INTO DARKNESS AND THE MOON INTO BLOOD, BEFORE THE GREAT AND GLORIOUS DAY OF THE LORD SHALL COME. AND IT SHALL BE THAT EVERYONE WHO CALLS ON THE NAME OF THE LORD WILL BE SAVED.'…Jesus the Nazarene, a man attested…by God with miracles and wonders and signs which God performed through Him…this *Man*…nailed to a cross by the hands of godless men…put *Him* to death…This Jesus God raised up again…Therefore having been exalted to the right hand of God, and having received from the Father the promise of the Holy Spirit, He has poured forth this which you both see and hear" (Acts 2:14, 16-23, 32-33).

According to this, the last days began the day Jesus set foot on this earth and rose from the dead to ascend back into heaven. It's not like the year two thousand marked the beginning of the last days, or the year we're in now, or even any other year to come. The Book of Acts says that all the way back in the First Century the last days were upon the world. Does this mean another one or two thousand years could pass before the wrath of God brings about the newness of life? The Bible makes a couple things clear about this. One, "For you yourselves know full well that the day of the Lord will come just like a thief in the night. While they are saying, 'Peace and safety!' then destruction will come upon them suddenly like labor pains upon a woman with child, and they will not escape" (1 Thessalonians 5:2-3). Two, Jesus said that, "Heaven and earth will pass away…But of that day and hour no one knows, not even the angels of heaven, nor the Son, but the Father alone" (Matthew 24:35-36). God through His word is making it clear that I won't know until the moment it happens. I'm also relieved that I don't need to know either. We just read that no one knows when the Lord will return nor when the final day of the world will truly be.

So maybe it's just this simple. These are the last days, and God has reserved the knowledge of the final hour for Himself. This actually frees me from trying to figure out whenever or whatever the end of the world is. I get the sense that there is no point in spending my thought, energy, or worry, pining away about knowing what day God has appointed to change reality as we know it. Now realizing this, the real concern I have are people who say they know when the end is because "God" told them so. After reading in the Bible that, "no one knows" how can any human being proclaim this knowledge, and how could people believe them? Perhaps signs of the time may point to the return of Christ more than in the past, but how can anyone ever justify stating a specific point in time when the end will be? It's a fact we're moving closer to the final day, every day. Again though, Jesus made it clear that no one knows the hour except "the Father alone."

That's as far as I need to go with this. Aside from the fact the Bible makes clear there is an "end," speculation about the last hour is virtually pointless because of the fact that God has made it clear that none of us can know. Unfortunately it's been demonstrated throughout history that individuals known and unknown have claimed to be God, or Christ, or someone that has come to save us who in fact weren't. I've even met a person or two on the streets of San Francisco who thought they were God, and it was apparent to me they were mentally ill. So for the sake of clarity, I really want to verify the Bible's position about false prophets. I'm sure I'm not the only person out here completely disturbed when people are led down the path of deception with end-of-the-world speculations to the point of mind control or even to death.

The words of Jesus stress: "Beware of the false prophets, who come to you in sheep's clothing, but inwardly are ravenous wolves. You will know them by their fruits. Grapes are not gathered from thorn *bushes* nor figs from thistles, are they? So every good tree bears good fruit, but the bad tree bears bad fruit. A good tree cannot produce bad fruit, nor can a bad tree produce good fruit" (Matthew 7:15-18). We are being instructed by Jesus to examine the results of people's lives to help discern who they are and their intentions. There's literally no excuse for me being fooled about someone proclaiming the end of the world. The answer is clear—no one knows. I realize I am repeating myself, but I'm amazed how this can be forgotten so quickly and charlatans can be followed.

John, the disciple of Jesus who also wrote the Book of Revelation helps us to identify when someone is trying to trick us. He wrote, "Beloved, do not believe every spirit, but test the spirits to see whether they are from God, because many false prophets have gone out into the world. By this you will know the Spirit of God: every spirit that confesses that Jesus Christ has come in the flesh is from God; and every spirit that does not confess Jesus, is not from God; this is the *spirit* of the antichrist, of which you have heard that it is coming…They are from the world; therefore they speak *as* from the world, and the world listens to them. We are from God; he who knows God listens to us; he who is not from God does not listen to us. By this we know the spirit of truth and the spirit of error" (1 John 4:1-6). John is reminding us that the antichrist is coming, but even John does not say when. It was this same John who wrote the Book of Revelation, yet he only saw in concept what was to come. He gave no specific date. In the meantime God gives us license to test the makeup of people and certain situations so as not to be deceived. One of the defining characteristics of recognizing the Spirit of God is when Christ as Lord is confessed, but even this is to be confirmed by their "fruit."

I think humility is the best path to take with the issue of the end of the world. I'm humbled that I don't know, will never know, and genuinely don't have to. Many answers are available to us, which set this record straight. Although it's easier said than done, I am able to avoid deception altogether by studying the Bible and knowing what's true to begin with. Jesus said, "For many will come in My name, saying, 'I am the Christ,' and will mislead many. You will be hearing of wars and rumors of wars. See that you are not frightened, for *those things* must take place, but *that* is not yet the end" (Matthew 24:5-6). Attempts to deceive us will be made. This is to be expected, but God calls me to be prepared and skillful.

Jesus said, "Behold, I send you out as sheep in the midst of wolves; so be shrewd as serpents and innocent as doves" (Matthew 10:16). It's great to know I don't have to be a pushover or easy prey to situations in life that seek to take their advantage of me. I'm guided by God to live strategically with great intention. "…[W]e are no longer to be children, tossed here and there by waves and carried about by every wind of doctrine, by the trickery of men, by craftiness in deceitful scheming" (Ephesians 4:14). For this reason I want a sharp mind to worship God with so that my heart, soul, and strength will not be misled. God is calling me to use my mind to think, and to reason things out. It's liberating to be authorized to examine the Bible and every other thing seeking to influence my intellect. It's actually helpful to be bold.

Even in being highly prepared to detect false prophets and deceptive situations, it's still alarming that, "…for even Satan disguises himself as an angel of light. Therefore it is not surprising if his servants also disguise themselves as servants of righteousness, whose end will be according to their deeds" (2 Corinthians 11:14-15). It seems like Satan has an unfair advantage, because even evil is able to appear as needed enlightenment. It can be so hard to recognize deception. The best way I see to identify a counterfeit is to know what's genuine. So as long as Jesus is intimately sought out at the deepest levels, the devil's deceptions will have less and less advantage.

Anything trying to exalt itself above the knowledge of God tips me off as being intentionally (or potentially) deceitful. I think of entertainment and how I've got to be mindful not to casually chalk things up as mere amusement or clever ideas when they could be the devices of evil working to deceive me. It is clear that evil is extremely cunning. The Book of Proverbs contains countless principles that juxtapose right with wrong, good with evil, so that I can understand the ways of God and the tactics of the devil. I get the strong sense that Satan desires to take as much life into hell as possible.

The whole idea of false prophets seems so archaic to me in this day and age, but I still see people being misled by spiritual leaders. I also realize we have the option not to be. It appears obvious that there will always be people deceiving other people. Maybe the aim of the adversary is just to get people jaded enough not to care, to go on living life according to the desires of self, in place of the redemption of Christ and principles of God. And when we're all good and jaded, evil strikes hard with deception. The preventative measure is to be as familiar with the truth as humanly possible so as to quickly identify the counterfeits in life.

When it comes to the end of the world, I think false prophets are trying to get people focused on "when" God will act more so than "how" God directs us to live while we wait. This is why I think it's not really about when Christ will return anyway. It's really all about how we live today. The only question of concern I keep asking myself is, "What will I be doing with my life the day God comes to judge?" While we wait for Him the more important questions stand: What are my purposes? What are the things God is calling me to do today? Who can I be helping? What will I say to God when standing before Him, if I'm able to say anything? I'm working on these answers as my preoccupation—not trying to predict the end of the world. In light of this, when someone proclaims to know the "end" there's no reason to be fooled because we already know they speak out of place. Jesus said not to have fear of anyone other than God: "Do not fear those who kill the body but are unable to kill the soul; but rather fear Him who is able to destroy both soul and body in hell" (Matthew 10:28). Commitment to God shadows everything—even false prophets.

The Harvest of God

While we wait for God we can live for God. The Bible articulates there is much to be done on this earth. "…'The harvest is plentiful, but the workers are few. Therefore beseech the Lord of the harvest to send out workers into His harvest" (Matthew 9:37-38). The Lord invites us to participate in drawing together all people to God. The preparation of every soul is in process. Drawing ourselves to God is the great undertaking.

My outlook about the end of the world is one of hope in Christ. For this reason doom and gloom should not mark our days. It is very apparent God is offering hope and life. Sure, our world could change in a heartbeat—for better or for worse. As long as we're in a relationship with Christ and living for God, eternal life is assured. So what should we be troubled by? Beyond this, what I see mattering most is how we will live today, which leads into tomorrow and the next day, until the Lord chooses to change things. My new perspective is to live as if the end were tomorrow, yet plan as though His coming will be thousands of years from now. In Mark's Gospel account, Jesus told a parable describing the end: "…'The kingdom of God is like a man who casts seed upon the soil…when the crop permits, he immediately puts in the sickle, because the harvest has come" (Mark 4:26, 29).

The Apostle John also accounts something similar in the Book of Revelation, "Then I looked, and behold, a white cloud, and sitting on the cloud *was* one like a son of man, having a golden crown on His head and a sharp sickle in His hand. And another angel came out of the temple, crying with a loud voice to Him who sat on the cloud, 'Put in your sickle and reap, for the hour to reap has come, because the harvest of the earth is ripe. Then He who sat on the cloud swung His sickle over the earth, and the earth was reaped" (Revelation 14:14-16). These two passages of Scripture tell us that with each passing day the "harvest" of the earth approaches. There is undoubtedly a day coming that will mark the end when Jesus will reap the earth. The Book of Revelation describes what God will then bring:

"Then I saw a new heaven and a new earth; for the first heaven and the first earth passed away, and there is no longer *any* sea. And I saw the holy city, new Jerusalem, coming down out of heaven from God, made ready as a bride adorned for her husband. And I heard a loud voice from the throne, saying, 'Behold, the tabernacle of God is among men, and He will dwell among them, and they shall be His people, and God Himself will be among them, and He will wipe away every tear from their eyes; and there will no longer be *any* death; there will no longer be *any* mourning, or crying, or pain; the first things have passed away. And He who sits on the throne said, 'Behold, I am making all things new.' And He said, 'Write, for these words are faithful and true.' Then He said to me, 'It is done. I am the Alpha and the Omega, the beginning and the end. I will give to the one who thirsts from the spring of the water of life without cost. He who overcomes will inherit these things, and I will be his God and he will be My son. But for the cowardly and unbelieving and abominable and murderers and immoral persons and sorcerers and idolaters and all liars, their part *will be* in the lake that burns with fire and brimstone, which is the second death" (Revelation 21:1-8).

It's difficult to fathom this vision of things to come! It's hard for me to believe that this will be a reality some day. Part of me is apprehensive to think how such events will transpire if they are in fact scheduled in my lifetime, but I trust God more and more that everything will work out according to His plan. I've heard debate among scholars and theologians as to exactly how they think the Bible says we'll get to the point in time when the new heaven and earth arrive. Some say God will take all those who call Him "Lord" before the "great tribulation" of the world which has been prophesied; some say during; and some even say after. There's even debate over what events in the Book of Revelation and prophecies of the Bible have already been fulfilled. I don't even want to begin imagining what the great tribulation will be like. Again, the Bible sets me free from worrying about "when," because I don't need to know—I can't know. But to those who long for the end of the world and the judgment of God, the Bible says this: "Alas, you who are longing for the day of the LORD, For what purpose *will* the day of the LORD *be* to you? It *will be* darkness and not light. *Will* not the day of the Lord *be* darkness instead of light, Even gloom with no brightness in it?" (Amos 5:18, 20).

My whole point is to not get caught up in "end of the world" matters. I don't know that anyone should be longing for the end of the world, let alone be trying to predict it. That day will take care of itself. Earlier on we read about Jesus telling us not to worry about tomorrow. For all people, the end should not be the concern, but the beginning of life in relationship with God is. The *time* of the "end" is pale in comparison to how we live life today. Who then should be concerned? Whatever distress we may have can be resolved by going to God. If we fear for someone we love, pray for his or her soul. We can go to them and share our love and God's love with them. We can help meet each other's to meet practical needs, and in so doing demonstrate the Spirit of God.

We can turn our attention to the Holy Spirit and ask for strength and assurance through Christ. We can ask the Spirit of God to dwell within us. The future does not require fretting about. Today is at hand. The One who is coming in wrath against evil is reaching for us with love this very moment. This is the truth, based on the foundation of those who walked with Jesus and died so long ago to reach the ends of the earth with this message from heaven. I observe that God is reaching still through the sign upon Half Dome. There is much to live for—an eternity to look forward to. Today, we should focus on our relationship with God and how to make planet earth a better, healthier place.

About the Work of the Lord

"...[D]o not be worried about your life, *as to* what you will eat or what you will drink; nor for your body, *as to* what you will put on. Is not life more than food, and the body more than clothing? Look at the birds of the air, that they do not sow, nor reap nor gather into barns, and *yet* your heavenly Father feeds them. Are you not worth much more than they? And who of you by being worried can add a *single* hour to his life? And why are you worried about clothing? Observe how the lilies of the field grow; they do not toil nor do they spin, yet I say to you that not even Solomon in all his glory clothed himself like one of these. But if God so clothes the grass of the field, which is *alive* today and tomorrow is thrown into the furnace, *will He* not much more *clothe* you? You of little faith! Do not worry then, saying, 'What will we eat?' or 'What will we drink?' or 'What will we wear for clothing?'...for your heavenly Father knows that you need all these things. But seek first His kingdom and His righteousness, and all these things will be added to you. So do not worry about tomorrow; for tomorrow will care for itself. Each day has enough trouble of its own" (Matthew 6:25-34).

The principle of first seeking the kingdom of God is how I started spending my time after high school. I sought God and was provided with the paramount answers, and my purposes. I trusted God for the truth about my life and I was shown answers through Half Dome. I was set free to have confidence about the future.

Reading this passage reminds me that seeking the kingdom of God will more than meet my needs. As long as I'm working with and not against God, I have assurance that I will not lack what I need and even more so, prosper in blessing.

In reading not to worry about my provision, I don't get the idea that I'm free from being responsible either. Good stewardship is part of all this. I shouldn't let worry permeate my spirit. The Bible teaches, "Be anxious for nothing, but in everything by prayer and supplication with thanksgiving let your requests be made known to God. And the peace of God, which surpasses all comprehension, will guard your hearts and your minds in Christ Jesus" (Philippians 4:6-7). The goal here is having peace as I work, because God isn't giving a pass for neglecting responsibilities. The Apostle Paul wrote, "…if anyone is not willing to work, then he is not to eat, either" (2 Thessalonians 3:10). I am "willing."

I am to seek peace and work to meet my needs, as the Bible makes reference to: "…work in quiet fashion and eat [my] own bread" (2 Thessalonians 3:12). Jesus' point in "not worrying" was to not lose sleep over matters of obtaining the things I in fact work for. Living by faith day to day as to what my future will be is something I strive for (though easier said than done). In light of this, worry and speculation about the future should not consume, nor distract us from fulfilling our purposes. Instead, I'm called to spend time seeking the kingdom of God and doing acts that manifest the kingdom and its goodness. God will provide things to us in order to help accomplish the heavenly purposes on earth.

"Therefore…present your bodies a living and holy sacrifice, acceptable to God, *which is* your spiritual service of worship" (Romans 12:1). This scripture tells me that sacrificial death is not a requirement to please God. Jesus did this in our place. God now wants me to live for Jesus. God gives us life so we can in turn live for God. This ignites my soul with passion to help make the earth realm the place God intends.

I see living for God as being as important as dying for God—if not more so. The Bible assures, "for if we live, we live for the Lord, or if we die, we die for the Lord; therefore whether we live or die, we are the Lord's. For to this end Christ died and lived again, that He might be Lord both of the dead and of the living" (Romans 14:8-9). "Finally, be strong in the Lord and in the strength of His might" (Ephesians 6:10). "…for He Himself has said, 'I WILL NEVER DESERT YOU, NOR WILL

I EVER FORSAKE YOU,' so that we confidently say, 'THE LORD IS MY HELPER, I WILL NOT BE AFRAID. WHAT WILL MAN DO TO ME?'" (Hebrews 13:5-6). I am free to live life to the fullest! God's hold is eternal. What then should I fear except letting go of God? I must place firm hold onto God, yet I will fail at times to do this. But my hope is in Christ Jesus for what He has already done—what no one else could do. Jesus said, "…in Me you may have peace. In the world you have tribulation, but take courage; I have overcome the world" (John 16:33).

Storming the Gates of Hell

I remember back to when I graduated high school, and set out on the search to know the truth about life—whether God existed. I wanted to know for certain the true priorities. And now I do. My relationship with God is priority over all else, directing me to love others with the heart of Jesus. This road I'm traveling reveals my relationship with God and others as the most important aspect of life. Being secure in Jesus is the only assurance of my eternal existence. My uncertainty about what truly matters most is now crystal clear.

Upon me writing my account, the images upon Half Dome are being released to our generation. Through this stone wall I sense God challenging us and the generations to come, to be known for resolving the truth about God, awakening a spirit of unity and service for the kingdom of God to love and serve the world. Let this place in time be associated with people who seek the power of God to move mountains out of our way—who turn the hearts of fathers toward God and toward their families and children. Let this generation be healed from monetary debt, and be remembered for its love and charitable giving to the widows and orphans, the hungry, the sick, and the oppressed. Let us put away the pride of self and vanity and materialism, and choose the spirit of humility. Let us fervently engage the Holy Bible and examine it with all diligence, examining our own spirit. Let this be how we spend the time until Christ returns. Even if this generation passes away, let this be the model our descendants know to follow.

John 3:16-18 helps us understand what trust in Jesus means. John 5:8-9 confirms that each one of us has sinned, but that Christ died for us to save us from the wrath of God. Romans 10:9 leads me to salvation: "…if you confess with your mouth Jesus *as* Lord, and believe in your heart that God raised Him from the dead, you will be saved." 1 John 1:9 also verifies: "If we confess our sins, He is faithful and righteous to forgive us our sins and to cleanse us from all unrighteousness. If we say that we have not sinned, we make Him a liar and His word is not in us." I know that God led me to this point through the significance of His sign upon Half Dome and through my search of the Holy Bible I know that the Resurrection of Christ explains it all. The rest amounts to following Jesus.

Jesus proclaimed the great commission upon His resurrection, "…'All authority has been given to Me in heaven and on earth. Go therefore and make disciples of all the nations, baptizing them in the name of the Father and the Son and the Holy Spirit, teaching them to observe all that I commanded you; and lo, I am with you always, even to the end of the age'" (Matthew 28:18-20). Regarding "what time it was" Jesus told his disciples back then, "…'It is not for you to know times or epochs which the Father has fixed by His own authority; but you will receive power when the Holy Spirit has come upon you; and you shall be My witnesses both in Jerusalem, and in all Judea and Samaria, and even to the remotest part of the earth" (Acts 1:7-8).

This opportunity to constructively influence our world and culture stands ready to engage. Christ encourages us to, "Let your light shine before men in such a way that they may see your good works, and glorify your Father who is in heaven" (Matthew 5:16). I truly feel that we are meant to share the truth with others. We should be encouraged to tell our story about how God is touching us. Share the things guiding you to God. Be bold! Let's rise up and live life for all it's worth—for Christ! Our world is ultimately under One God with Jesus as the common ground. Do you see with me the Rock of Salvation reaching for us? Let's reach to God.

Being Alert

God has been preparing for a gathering of souls the world has not yet seen. It's written that, "[I]n a moment, in the twinkling of an eye, at the last trumpet; for the trumpet will sound, and the dead will be raised imperishable, and we will be changed" (1 Corinthians 15:52). Jesus taught to be prepared and alert in regards to the end. He told a story to describe how it will be when God calls those who are waiting at the end of this world:

"Then the kingdom of heaven will be comparable to ten virgins, who took their lamps and went out to meet the bridegroom. Five of them were foolish, and five were prudent. For when the foolish took their lamps, they took no oil with them, but the prudent took oil in flasks along with their lamps. Now while the bridegroom was delaying, they all got drowsy and *began* to sleep. But at midnight there was a shout, 'Behold, the bridegroom! Come out to meet *him.*' Then all those virgins rose and trimmed their lamps. The foolish said to the prudent, 'Give us some of your oil, for our lamps are going out.' But the prudent answered, 'No, there will not be enough for us and you *too;* go instead to the dealers and buy *some* for yourselves.' And while they were going away to make the purchase, the bridegroom came, and those who were ready went in with him to the wedding feast; and the door was shut. Later the other virgins also came, saying, 'Lord, lord, open up for us.' But he answered, 'Truly I say to you, I do not know you.' Be on the alert then, for you do not know the day nor the hour" (Matthew 25:1-13).

In light of this, just about the only things we can do in regards to the end of the world is to prepare by trusting in Jesus for rescue, and be ready for the day when God will "shout." Tomorrow could be the hour God set to be the last. Perhaps in a thousand years, but we just don't know. I remember what the Apostle Paul wrote: "For you yourselves know full well that the day of the Lord will come just like a thief in the night" (1 Thessalonians 5:2). The Apostle Peter confirmed: "...the day of the Lord will come like a thief, in which the heavens will pass away with a roar and the elements will be destroyed with intense heat, and the earth and its works will be burned up" (2 Peter 3:10). Time will suddenly cease. God will "roar" as His image upon Half Dome depicts. But in the end it will be the actual reverberation to our marrow, rather than a still mark upon this stone wall. Jesus described that day this way:

"For the coming of the Son of Man will be just like the days of Noah. For as in those days before the flood they were eating and drinking, marrying and giving in marriage, until the day that Noah entered the ark, and did not understand until the flood came and took them all away; so will the coming of the Son of Man be. Then there will be two men in the field; one will be taken and one will be left. Two women *will be* grinding at the mill; one will be taken and one will be left. Therefore be on the alert, for you do not know which day your Lord is coming. But be sure of this, that if the head of the house had known at what time of the night the thief was coming, he would have been on the alert and would not have allowed his house to be broken into. For this reason you also must be ready; for the Son of Man is coming at an hour when you do not think *He will*. Who then is the faithful and sensible slave whom his master put in charge of his household to give them their food at the proper time? Blessed is that slave whom his master finds so doing when he comes. Truly I say to you that he will put him in charge of all his possessions. But if that evil slave says in his heart, 'My master is not coming for a long time,' and begins to beat his fellow slaves and eat and drink with drunkards; the master of that slave will come on a day when he does not expect *him* and at an hour which he does not know, and will cut him in pieces and assign him a place with the hypocrites; in that place there will be weeping and gnashing of teeth" (Matthew 24:37-51).

Faithful and sensible hearts will anticipate the hour, and will not be afraid of God. Those engaged in oppressive actions will be struck with panic. Destruction will come upon those who abuse their neighbors. Those who show cruelty to the ones God purposed as aid to the afflicted will be devastated. The hour of wrath continues its stride. The coming of the Lord approaches all. What will our response be today?

The anticipation of Christ's return builds. The Lord upon Half Dome foreshadows the mighty shout signifying His return: "For the Lord Himself will descend from heaven with a shout, with the voice of *the* archangel and with the trumpet of God, and the dead in Christ will rise first. Then we who are alive and remain will be caught up together with them in the clouds to meet the Lord in the air, and so we shall always be with the Lord. Therefore comfort one another with these words" (1 Thessalonians 4:16-18).

Jesus in the Revelation of John was recorded as saying, "Behold, I am coming quickly, and My reward *is* with Me, to render to every man according to what he has done. I am the Alpha and the Omega, the first and the last, the beginning and the end" (Revelation 22:12-13). The author of the Book of Hebrews wrote, "Let us hold fast the confession of our hope without wavering, for He who promised is faithful; and let us consider how to stimulate one another to love and good deeds, not forsaking our own assembling together, as is the habit of some, but encouraging *one another;* and all the more as you see the day drawing near" (Hebrews 10:23-25).

In part I struggle to even imagine God coming with a "shout" and people physically ascending into the air to meet the Lord. Though doubt knocks at the doorstep of my spirit, I remind myself God can do anything. This foretold reality is spoken for by this present reality manifested in Scripture and granite. It may seem like a fictional story, yet it's entirely true. It's all right to wrestle with, but at the end of the day I align with the truth. There is security in His coming: "This is the promise which He Himself made to us: eternal life…Now, little children, abide in Him, so that when He appears, we may have confidence and not shrink away from Him in shame at His coming" (1 John 2:25, 28).

"Therefore, be on the alert—for you do not know when the master of the house is coming, whether in the evening, at midnight, or when the rooster crows, or in the morning—in case he should come suddenly and find you asleep. What I say to you I say to all, 'Be on the alert!'" (Mark 13:35-37). It could just be on an ordinary day that God would choose to change life, as we know it. Jesus said to be on the alert.

Epilogue

It's been almost fifteen years since my initial encounter at the foot of Half Dome. Writing this book was truly an experience governed by life changes spanning the years. My initial encounter in Yosemite started with seeing two images from the valley floor, and led to the many more over time upon closer and closer study. I went from having uncertainty about whether God even existed, to physically sensing a supernatural presence, to ultimately witnessing an amazing revelation that Jesus is God. Eventually I committed myself to a church body when I was twenty-four, volunteering, and maturing through biblical teaching, while at the same time building invaluable relationships along the way. It was a great challenge and life-altering experience, which I am still benefiting from the fruits of that labor to this day.

In essence, the whole time I spent writing this book I've been learning how to love and be loved. I met my wife Stephani at a weekly church gathering held on Saturday nights called "The Round Table", led by Pastor Ron H. It provided a way to learn about the Bible, and socialize with the people within our community. Meeting Stephani has greatly changed my life for the better, and our new family has begun its new chapter. And yes, after we were married we made that trip to North Dome and shared an awesome night out under the stars, up in the air above the valley floor. Amazingly enough, this hike happened to be her first backpack trip too.

Since my days of installing hardwood floors, I have gone on to sell flooring products and projects in the San Francisco Bay Area. I have learned that you can't go wrong working hard, and that doing the right thing for people is really what matters most. Everything else in turn will work itself out over time. I've also learned that successful business can equate to an abundance of family time, making for both true health and wellness. I think just about any customer appreciates this personal quality in who they do business with.

My commitment to Christ has been steadfast ever since the Spirit of God revealed these images to me in Yosemite Valley. Throughout the last fourteen years, my heart for the Lord has been on fire, cold, and even lukewarm at times. I wish my heart would be all of what God desires for me, but fortunately, my relationship is real. I still have much to learn about being intimate with God, so I keep striving to mature in this way. I sense a renewed strength in presenting this book to you, as a new season of life begins to take hold. The whole process of writing this book has demonstrated to me how easily and rapidly time passes.

I am able to better relate with the process the Apostles went through in scribing their thoughts to account for their time spent with Jesus on earth. I used to think, "Why didn't they just "hammer out" their account of their life-changing encounter with God? Why did it take them so many years to write their Gospels and Epistles?" Then I remind myself that they didn't even have a computer with a spell and grammar checker—they had to handwrite everything, nor was it with a nice ballpoint pen and smooth white paper. They didn't have a copy machine or printing press. Plus having to hold down a job for their sustenance—ten, twenty, or even thirty years of writing under their circumstances seems entirely reasonable to finally publish their account of someone so monumental as Jesus. Under the conditions, I think they actually did pretty well. I now understand that this kind of writing is not just a report but also a calling—a calling to take the precious time to process and share the magnitude of such events and experiences. Time not only tests the elements of that for which we write about, it also tests our commitment to what we've written. To still be living according to the past events that initially changed us sequentially bears witness to the writings themselves. The passage of time itself actually becomes part of the story.

I've been back to Yosemite many times since that first day I stepped foot onto that valley floor. It's been one way of taking in the grandeur of God. I've come to know that this place possesses a depth only God can reveal to us. To this day, I still discover amazing features on that rock. Recently, during Christmas I watched the sun rise and set on Half Dome, via the Internet from home. Storms rolled in and out of the Valley, and the brilliant dance of light graced the face of Half Dome.

First light on Christmas morning.

Christmas sunrise from the Valley floor.

Waiting for the storm to pass at sunset, December 27th.

Sunset at 4:36p from Sentinel Dome, December 28th.

Sunset at 4:37pm from Turtle Dome, December 28th.

Sunset at 4:37pm from the Valley floor, December 28th.

These web cams at www.yosemite.org allow the different vantage points of Half Dome to be seen year round from just about any place in the world with a computer and a connection. I am always amazed to find features for the first time, which were present all along.

In 2006, the long hair of Christ shown itself to me as the work of art it has always been. I never before noticed the sculpted, rounded details of curls and locks of hair flowing down the top, left side of Half Dome. This truly displays the concentrated handiwork of the One Who also created the universe.

The search became a journey, leading to my ongoing personal transformation. Through it all I see that life is about giving, helping, and sacrificing in the name of love. I am now part of an Assemblies of God church community. Our family gives our finances in faith for what God is doing through people in our local body. We are helping to participate, as we are able. In turn our church contributes to the global ministries throughout the world. My wife and I appreciate the solid foundation that the Assemblies of God provides the multitude of congregations associated with it.

We are also part of a small home group that meets once a week to study the Bible and pray for one another. My wife and I were invited to be a part of this group many years ago, which has consisted of about ten people or so. We also go to different churches of different denominations. Our weekly gathering is both a needed strength and valuable resource to our family. We've grown to love and appreciate everyone in it. I also think this is what was taking place in my dream when I was seeing the multitudes of people going in and out of the houses spread across the land. It wasn't a "door to door" strategy to "evangelize." The essence of the dream scene was about what was going on inside each home: an intimate gathering in the name of Jesus initiated by someone's personal invitation to come in. This type of gathering represents the heart of church. It's out of desire and not obligation that we meet—to grow in Christ and know one another.

Crown Financial Ministries is a great ongoing ministry that has been a tool, personally impacting our family for the better. It teaches Biblically based financial principles about how to steward over personal resources and shows the way to debt-free living. Crown wants people to have a more intimate relationship with Christ, and to see their God-given purposes fulfilled. We practice many of the principles espoused by Crown, and continue to be successful in debt-free living.

The Salvation Army is another organization we trust our time and financial resources with to help support the work of angels. They are very efficient, and reach people with not only the love of Christ, but with the practical means as well—food, clothing, and shelter. We are mindful of the integrity these organizations demonstrate. They are being responsible to steward, with the heart of God on earth, the time and resources of others offered in faith.

Initially, my church experience started in a body vibrant with growth, exuding passion and teaching to help people understand who Jesus is. Eventually I became concerned about certain practices and left to find another church home. I began to recognize an "inward focus" toward itself. This was evident in the apprehension of the leaders to approve of people relocating somewhere else to employ different personal callings in God. I perceived a fear in the church leadership of letting people go because it meant losing someone's service, which would need to be replaced. From the leadership's perspective it seemed to always be "God's will" that someone stay. However, when the church grew to be much bigger, people relocating suddenly became a "non-issue." This confirmed the overall hesitation to equip or invest relationally in people who were thought would potentially move away—not out of church, just to a different one. The preference was to spend time with people who intended to stay indefinitely. This spoke to me that we were missing the point to trust that the whole church is the Lord's to do what He intends with anyone, whether they'd be staying or going from this one church body.

Church bylaws and financial statements were also not openly shared with the congregation there. In addition, intentionally in a quiet manner, the church leadership held both Oneness Pentecostalism and Trinitarian viewpoints as it pertains to the Godhead. I'm not saying I myself completely comprehend the nature and science of the mysterious Godhead, but I came to conclude that it's not healthy to avoid the issue either. Even institutions of higher learning would agree that healthy church leadership does not keep its congregation in the dark about its own doctrine of the Godhead, letting people think they are part of a certain type of denomination when in fact the church's true philosophical position is something ambiguous.

The reason I feel the need to share my experience is due to the fact that far too many people who genuinely love and seek God are skeptical of church. Some reasons are definitely due to people choosing to avoid church altogether because of sin in their life, but even this choice is somewhat faulty. There has never been a single Christian in the world that manages to be sinless—maybe sinning less, but not sinless. Churches would literally be empty if we all stayed out because of our sin. Our sin is one very big reason church is meant to support us. The legitimate concern I do have is that enough church bodies aren't adhering to true Biblical doctrine, and that people who desire a relationship with God are avoiding church for this reason. Unbiblical church structures ultimately represent deceit, and people eventually detect the deception and become turned off to church altogether. Maybe it's not entirely intentional of church bodies that falter here, but there are definite problems that need resolving. As a result, too many people are missing out on the blessing of God's church He purposed it to be.

In light of these things, even though many people are choosing to avoid God's church, church is nevertheless something God wants us connected through. So if you're like me you don't want to be duped, or be part of something nonsensical, unreasonable, or just plain silly. You want church to be powerful and alive. We want it to be honest and real for heaven's sake! My own experience over many years has led me to learn much of what a Biblical church looks like, and how to find a healthy church. At the very least, church home groups (or cells) have been the foundational meeting place of people seeking Christ since the very first Christian gathering (read the Book of Acts). Home gatherings that authentically center on the person of Christ are the true heart of what church is all about. Jesus said, "For where two or three have gathered together in My name, I am there in their midst" (Matthew 18:20). The greater church body becomes that much stronger when we are a healthy part of it, and by healthy I mean individually identifying truth and committing to accurately understanding Biblical doctrine as we move to serve and love the world.

I'm really not trying to "sell" church here. My hope is that we will all better understand how to receive the empowerment that the Holy Spirit desires to give us. Whether it's spiritual, physical, financial, or relational, God desires to equip us with the means to fulfill His purposes and destiny for our lives. A healthy church is one major and vital way God essentially provides blessing through so that we who receive the blessing may in turn send it from our church to people around the world. Multitudes on earth are hoping and praying for God's blessing to be delivered to them, and church is a vehicle God practically works through.

My initial experience in Yosemite had me wondering if church is something God ultimately requires for my salvation. I questioned if it was mandatory that I attend. Eventually through my study of the Bible, it became clear we are saved by God's grace alone. For salvation, we can do nothing for God or ourselves. He has already done it all for us on the cross. Therefore, the gift of salvation is given to us through our confession and trust in the Lord Jesus, because of Who He is and what He has done. I therefore do not attend church for my salvation. I commit to church to be spiritually nourished and to help encourage others. My own church experience over the years proves to help me grow in Christ. So what I am getting at here? I'm saying to study the Bible and become more intimate with God and learn about our relationship with God, with others, and even with our self. The appendix at the end of this book references scriptures pertaining to the many aspects of church and leadership. I'm saying do not be deceived, and possess a clear understanding about essential Biblical doctrine. Continue your investigation of reality so you will fulfill the purposes God created in you.

I recently typed "what does a healthy church look like" into my internet search engine. I found many good resources laying out the structure for a healthy, Biblical church community. Healthy churches definitely exist today. This recent internet search helped shed further light on what God intends His church to be. We live in an age of information where guidance is plentiful. In fact, so much so that great care must be taken to examine everything in light of the Bible and reality to identify what's genuine. We shouldn't be afraid of the truth, and can embraced it because God is truth.

I do my best to live out Biblical principles, and when I fall short I lean on those around me to help set me straight. I used to think I was supposed to do it all by myself to demonstrate that I'm somehow a "successful, self-made man." In growing older with Godly humility, I realize that no one truthfully makes it in life alone. Rather, it's a blessing to be able to receive help and to walk with others through life. We all need each other. We are meant to carry one another. I have simply learned to acknowledge this, and in turn grow to appreciate the sacrificial love others want to give, and that I can give. God chooses to manifest His love for us this way, Jesus being the ultimate sacrifice who gave it all. I am happy and forever grateful for all God has done, and continues to do. May my life respond by never ceasing to follow after the One reality so boldly proclaims—Jesus!

Appendix

Bible scripture pertaining to aspects of church and leadership

Matthew 16:16-19

Ephesians 2:18-22

Acts 1:15, 23

Acts 5:1-11

1 Corinthians 11:2, 33-34

1 Corinthians 7:17

1 Thessalonians 1:6-8

2 Thessalonians 3:7-9

Acts 15:1-31

Acts 16:4-5

1 Corinthians 12:27-28

Ephesians 4:11-16

1 Corinthians 16:16

1 Corinthians 16:3

1 Timothy 3:8-13

Acts 14:23; 20:17, 28

1 Timothy 5:17-18

James 5:14

1 Timothy 3:2-7

Matthew 25:31-46

Matthew 18:15-18

Hebrews 10:23-25

1 Corinthians 1:10

Philippians 2:1-2

Ephesians3:14-21,4:1-6

1 Corinthians 10:16-17

Hebrews 13:17

Philippians 2:29

1 Corinthians 9:7-23

Philippians 4:10-18

1 Corinthians 15:1-7

Matthew 28:19-20

Matthew 5, 6, and 7

Luke 6:20-45

Mark 6:9-11

Mark 8:34-38

Matthew 18:21-22

Mark 12:29-31

John 13:34-35

Matthew 20:28

Luke 10:30-37

Mark 12:17

Mark 10:5-12

Matthew 24:42-51

Matthew 25:1-13

Mark 13:33-37

1 Timothy 3:8-10, 12

Galatians 6:7

1 Peter 5:2-3

Acts 20:28

1 Thessalonians 5:12-13

Philippians 3:17

1 Corinthians 14:33

1 Corinthians 14:40

Romans 16:17-18

2 Timothy 2:1-16

Philippians 2:25

2 Timothy 4:7

Philemon 2

1 Corinthians 8:7-13

James 1:27

John 21:15-17

Acts 5:15-16

Acts 6:7,11:21-22,14:1

Acts 2:41

Romans 12:4-5

1 Corinthians 12:12-27

Proverbs 27:17

Luke 13:24

Colossians 2:8

Matthew 10:26, 28

Titus 1:7-9

John 7:24

Mark 11:22-24

Luke 12:12

Acts 2:16-21

Romans 3:2

1 Corinthians 14:26

How to Order

Order securely online at www.thesignonhalfdome.com (preferred method)

Or send email to order@thesignonhalfdome.com

Or mail order to:

Attn: Order The Sign on Half Dome
Infinite Ripple
PO Box 27065
San Francisco, CA 94127

Customer information for email and mail orders

Name: _____

Quanity: _____

Credit Card type: _____

Credit Card number: _____

Card Expiration date: _____

Name on credit Card: _____

Phone number in case of questions: _____

Credit card billing address & mailing address (must be the same):

_____

_____

_____ Country:_____

For email and mail orders, please specify your shipping preference. Your account will be billed for the amount of your order plus shipping & handling. Shipping costs will range from 11% to 25% depending on method and location.

_____

comments: